PUB WALKS
IN
North Wales

THIRTY CIRCULAR WALKS
AROUND NORTH WALES INNS

Jim Knowles

D1249050

COUNTRYSIDE BOOKS
NEWBURY, BERKSHIRE

First Published 1994
© Jim Knowles 1994

Revised and updated 1999

COUNTRYSIDE BOOKS
3 Catherine Road
Newbury, Berkshire

ISBN 1 85306 314 2

Designed by Mon Mohan
Cover illustration by Colin Doggett
Photographs and maps by the author

Produced through MRM Associates Ltd., Reading
Typeset by Paragon Typesetters, Queensferry, Clwyd
Printed and bound in England by Woolnough Bookbinding,
Wellingborough

Contents

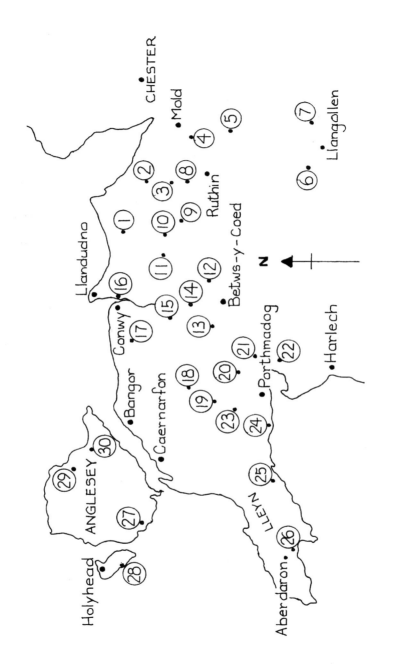

Area map showing locations of the walks.

Publisher's Note

We hope that you obtain considerable enjoyment from this book; great care has been taken in its preparation. However, changes of landlord and actual closures are sadly not uncommon. Likewise, although at the time of publication all routes followed public rights of way or well-established permitted paths, diversion orders can be made and permissions withdrawn.

We cannot accept responsibility for any inaccuracies, but we are anxious that all details covering both pubs and walks are kept up to date, and would therefore welcome information from readers which would be relevant to future editions.

Introduction

The area covered by this book stretches from near Llangollen in the east to Holyhead and Aberdaron in the far west. This encompasses a nation in miniature, the heartland of the Welsh language, and a region steeped in history. It stretches back to pre-historic times, through Celtic and Roman invasion, to the rise of the Welsh saints, to the Norman conquest, and the rivalry of the English and Welsh, to the Civil War, and on to the Industrial Revolution and modern times, with the impact of tourism.

The 30 walks outlined try, briefly, to point out some parts of this great historic canvas, covering 5,000 years. It is a picture set in a framework of great natural beauty. The sea, the towering mountains, lakes, forests, hills, valleys and rivers have all played their part. Now, in their own right, these natural features have become places that people visit to enjoy and refresh themselves.

Each walk is based on a pub that can also give refreshment, but of a different kind. The variety to be found in the 30 pubs chosen is as great as the variety of the countryside encountered. Here are pubs which have achieved the highest accolades in good food; ancient, and sometimes haunted pubs that were serving beer to people centuries ago, and remote village 'locals' that provide their own brand of hospitality and are 'different'.

Amongst this list are some that are bustling and busy in summer and quiet and restful in winter; others have a good trade all through the year, whilst others again, together with the school, the church or chapel, the post office and shop, provide a vital focal point in helping to keep their villages alive and flourishing – an issue of great importance to so many remote and small communities. All will offer a warm welcome, a good glass of beer and a variety of food to suit everyone's taste and appetite.

The average length of walk is just under 4 miles but there is a range from gentle strolls of under 3 miles to more strenuous walks of around 5 miles and, in some cases, up to 6 miles, if the extra, longer, routes described are undertaken. Most are easy going, especially if taken at a steady pace, but with some there are uphill stretches that will need to be taken slowly. Similarly, some walks cross open exposed country, and for these adequate gear should be taken. In almost every case it is best to wear good, waterproof footwear, preferably boots, as, even in the height of summer, there are stretches on many of the walks that can be wet.

Boots can create a problem with the pubs visited and, generally, it is better to take them off before going in, although there are a few pubs, in those areas popular with climbers and walkers, where they are prepared for boots. These pubs are mentioned. For those who find a walk incomplete without a dog, there is the vital need to ensure that livestock is not worried by them. Much of North Wales is devoted to sheep farming on open country and dog owners must keep dogs well in hand.

Many walkers have an interest in natural history and for them the variety of what may be seen and discovered along the way in North Wales is very great. I have made some comments about plants and birds particularly, but there will be much else to look at. Photographers, also, will not be disappointed by the potential good shots that will be encountered, not only where the views are concerned, impressive as they may be, but also old buildings, castles and the pubs themselves.

Jim Knowles

Preface to the 1999 Edition

I first met Jim Knowles some fourteen years ago, when he landed on our doorstep one day canvassing for his party as a councillor and ex-mayor of Aberconwy. He had walked up Nant-y-Gamar Road which goes on forever in a steep incline. He had also walked up our drive which also goes on forever in another steep incline (roughly over 400 yards) – everyone else drives up both places in their cars!

It was Jim who first stirred my interest in walking and so it was a privilege when I was asked to help with the revisions for this new edition of the book, following Jim's tragic death in 1997. I could think of no better memorial than to have it back on the book shelves.

It is now fully up to date again. However, some of the pub details have changed mainly because of the relaxation of the licensing laws that allow pubs previously 'dry' on a Sunday to open for business. A few amendments have also been necessary to the circuits themselves. Essentially, however, these are still the routes which Jim found so enjoyable and wanted to share with others.

Revising the book would not have been possible without assistance and I am greatly indebted to Gwen Williams for her vast knowledge of the area and for patiently reading the maps. Special thanks also go to Margery Ashcroft and Margaret Wood who accompanied us on many of the walks. I hope you will derive as much pleasure from them as we have.

As Jim said in his original introduction, the walks are all enjoyable, each one is different; they highlight the differences in the towns and villages of North Wales and the inns offer a very warm welcome to everyone who visits them.

Shirley Jones
Spring 1999

① Cwm
The Blue Lion

Tucked away in the wooded hills of Clwyd, the Blue Lion is a family-run business. The owners have retained and improved upon the high reputation for good food that the Blue Lion has had for many years, not only locally but much further afield. Accompanying the food, there is also available a fine selection of real ale and draught cider. Draught cask beers served are Worthington Best Bitter, Bass Mild and Guinness. There is also a guest beer available that varies weekly. Lagers include Pils and Carlsberg. However, whatever is being served, it is always good and a pleasure to drink, and the Blue Lion provides a warm and comfortable atmosphere in which to enjoy it.

Originally a 16th century farmhouse, the pub still retains throughout memories of its earlier origin – wooden beams, inglenook fireplaces with warm fires in the winter, as well as many interesting pieces of china and brass. A unique collection of over 200 chamber-pots hanging from the beams is not perhaps from the 16th century but always provides great interest! More in keeping with its age is the presence of the ghost of John Henry, a farmhand, reputed to have been murdered in 1646. He has been seen on occasions and has been blamed for several mysterious happenings in and around the building over the last few years. His name has been given to the pub's function room.

Sandwiches are not served, but there is a wide and excellent range of bar meals such as cottage pie, cooked 'provençale', available from the 'Gourmet Food Bar', and an extensive, help-yourself salad bar. The Blue Lion ice-creams are also famous. The Chambers restaurant is open for more formal dinners – reservations are requested. Two of the most popular dishes in the restaurant are caneton rotis Montmorency – a half freshly roasted duck in port and brandy sauce, garnished with black cherries; and fillet of beef Isabelle – prime fillet stuffed with a home-made Stilton mousse, topped with an artichoke and coated with a madeira sauce. The Blue Lion is open at lunchtime from 12 noon to 3 pm every day, except Mondays, opening again at 7 pm. Children are welcome at lunchtime but, in the evenings, the minimum age is 14. Outside there is a pleasant garden with seats and tables looking out across the Vale of Clwyd and here dogs can join their owners, if well behaved and on a lead, but not indoors.

Telephone: 01745 570733.

How to get there: Cwm is tucked away down narrow country lanes, quite close to both Rhuddlan and Dyserth. From the A5151 Holywell to Rhuddlan road, turn southwards at Dyserth along a lane to Cwm. Alternatively, turn off the A55(T) Chester to Bangor road on the approach to Rhuallt Hill and take the 'old road', marked Rhuallt and Tremeirchion. Turn northwards at Rhuallt, along the lane signposted to Cwm.

Parking: There is a spacious car park beside the Blue Lion, overlooked by a large dovecote.

Length of the walk: 4½ miles. Map: OS Landranger 116 Denbigh and Colwyn Bay (GR 066775).

Apart from a short, steep section, near the start, this is an easy walk through woods, along narrow, high-hedged lanes, so typical of Clwyd, and taking in a stretch of Offa's Dyke path. It is a walk which is suitable for all seasons, as the high hedges are a great protection on cold, blustery days, and it is dry underfoot. On the way there are magnificent views across the Vale of Clwyd, the mountains of Snowdonia and the coastal plain as well as over the Dee and Mersey towards Liverpool. Southwards the Berwyn mountains can be seen in the far distance. Offa's Dyke path is one of the national pathways, running from near Newport in Gwent, northwards to Prestatyn on the north coast. This path follows, as far as possible, the line of the rampart built in the 8th century by King Offa of Mercia in an attempt to define the 149-mile western frontier of Mercia. Whether to keep the English out of Wales or the Welsh out of England has been a point argued over ever since!

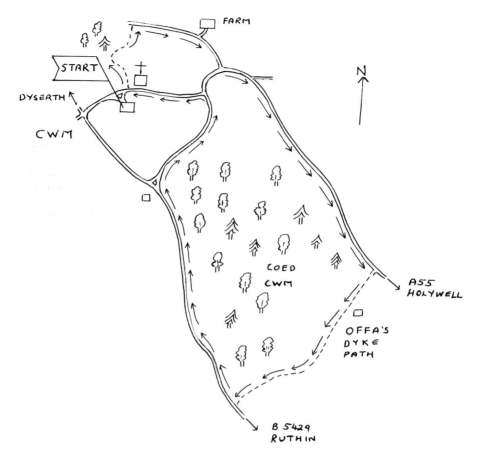

The Walk

From the Blue Lion, take the path just across the road, next to the gate to the church of St Mael and St Sulien. It was in this churchyard that an excavated grave revealed a skeleton lying on top of a coffin – thought by some to be connected with the murder of John Henry. The path runs along beside the churchyard wall as far as the graveyard, then it strikes out diagonally across the meadow towards the woods on a slightly raised causeway. This leads to a stile under a row of mature sycamore trees. Over this stile, the path through the wood is easy to follow as it rises steeply, crossing a stream and passing a cave with a brick lintel. Another stile is reached and, on the far side, an old cart track runs alongside a fence to a point where it joins a narrow lane. Turn right and walk up this lane. There are fine views of Liverpool Bay and the Great and Little Ormes, near Llandudno. From spring to autumn, these hedges are particularly full of a great variety of wild flowers and are a happy hunting ground for botanists.

At the junction, go right, then, shortly afterwards, go left, and then right again. This single-track lane climbs steadily uphill to Coed Cwm, with, this time, marvellous views to the east across the Dee and Mersey.

At the far end of the wood, which is on the right-hand side and about ¾ mile from the last junction, turn right on to Offa's Dyke path. This path is clearly marked, passing through hilltop country of gorse and hawthorn, now with panoramic views to the south. Initially a stony track, the path, after passing a small farm, becomes grassy. There are several stiles along this part of the route, which eventually reaches the southern corner of Coed Cwm. Climb the stile here and go quite steeply downhill through the woods to a point where another narrow lane is reached. Turn right and walk back towards Cwm. After about a mile, just as a group of houses is reached, bear right along a very narrow lane and follow it around to the Blue Lion.

2 Milwr
The Glan-yr-Afon

It is not every pub that is mentioned in the *Guinness Book of Records* but the Glan-yr-Afon's claim to fame is that when Mrs Mary Evans finally gave up running the pub in 1977 it had been directly connected with her family for 418 years. It is the longest continual tenancy ever recorded, from 1559 to 1977. The current owners keep up the tradition of providing a notable place for a drink and a meal.

The Glan-yr-Afon's position must be one of the finest in the country, as it looks out from the hillside above Holywell across the Dee estuary, with panoramic views to the Wirral and the Mersey beyond, and, beyond again, across large parts of Lancashire. The older part of the pub remains and, to capitalise on the view, a newer restaurant has been added, providing a stunning outlook. A new extension is currently being built to house seven en suite bedrooms and an extra bar which, it is hoped, will encourage even more walkers. The extension is due to open around September 1999, when new opening times will come into effect.

There are two extremely varied menus with a third being assembled at present. Bookings are advisable. Children are well catered for, not only in the playground outside but also in the family room next to the main bar.

The Glan-yr-Afon currently serves Webster's and Ruddles ales, and Foster's lager, with Strongbow cider also in the line up. The Glan-yr-Afon is part of a small group of pubs in this area dedicated to the real ale movement. Drinks can be enjoyed inside in the comfortable bar or, on a fine day, outside in the garden where the view can be surveyed at leisure.

The Glan-yr-Afon is open seven days a week from 12 noon to 2 pm for food (sometimes all afternoon depending on customers' requirements) and, in the evenings, every day except Monday, from 7 pm to 10 pm (Sundays 7 pm to 9 pm). Well behaved and leashed dogs can join their owners in the garden but not indoors.

The whole area around the Glan-yr-Afon was actively employed in lead mining, and, in fact, the pub is close to one of the main shafts. This industry has now long gone but the remnants can be seen everywhere and inside the pub there is a fascinating display of pictures, maps and plans of how it was at the height of the mining activity. It is only when you have seen this display that it is possible to realise the extent of the mining nearby and the effort that went into it, in what is now a quiet area.

Telephone: 01352 710052.

How to get there: Turn right off the old A55 Holywell to Chester road at the Calcot Arms (note that this is not the new A55(T) expressway) and go up the narrow road signposted for Milwr. The road goes uphill and on a right-hand bend just before the expressway overpass bridge turn left down to the Glan-yr-Afon. There is another turning to the right on the same A55 road about ½ mile further on, if the Calcot Arms turning is missed.

Parking: There is a large car park beside the Glan-yr-Afon.

Length of the walk: 4½ miles. Map: OS Landranger 116 Denbigh and Colwyn Bay (GR 196737).

The walk crosses Holywell Common and Halkyn mountain. The whole area was an active lead-mining centre but now little remains − the occasional old stone building, humpy spoil heaps, mostly covered in gorse and heather, and old, safely capped mine shafts. In modern times quarrying has taken over from mining as a local industry. Both Holywell Common and Halkyn mountain are noted places for plant life, orchids in particular, as well as for butterflies. Walking is pleasant and easy across this common land with fine views on clear days to the east and southwards to the Berwyn Mountains. The common is heavily grazed by sheep in parts, although this is good dog walking country.

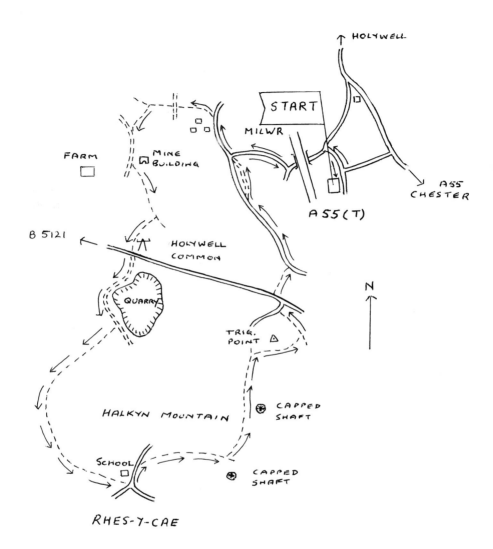

The Walk

From the Glan-yr-Afon turn left, then left again, going under the expressway overpass. On the far side, go right up the lane signposted for Brynford. A quarter of a mile further up, this lane comes out on Holywell Common at a T-junction. Turn right and, a few hundred yards further on, just after a sharp right-hand bend, take the grassy track to the left, which runs behind a group of three houses.

At the next fork, bear right and keep straight on. Cross over a stoney roadway running across the track and, about 300 yards further on, turn left downhill, along another track, which runs into a shallow valley. This joins with a stony cart track running uphill through a series of hillocks – the remains of old mine workings. At the top of this hill, an old stone building will be seen, more or less straight ahead. Keeping this building on the left, go along the grassy track which runs directly away from the farm which is close by. Several paths cross this track but, after about ¼ mile, take a right turn up a track which, after going over a hillock, passes very close by the base of an electricity pylon.

Shortly after, a road is reached. Across this road is the area known as Halkyn mountain. Many species of moorland birds can be seen on both Holywell Common and Halkyn mountain – stonechats, whinchats, linnets and goldfinches. Ravens, peregrine falcons and kestrels are also regularly seen here. On the other side of the road a stony track runs along the edge of a quarry which is hidden by a grassy bund. The track curves around, then bears left, still beside the bund. Further along, with the village of Rhes-y-Cae in sight, branch off down a broad, grassy track running off to the right. This curves around towards the village, across the heath.

Walk up to the houses. One of the first buildings reached is the small school, dated 1898. Beyond the school, turn left along the single-track road. Opposite the end of the playground, take the track to the right which again runs across the heath and heads towards a radio mast.

A few hundred yards further on the track divides. Go left, towards a clearly visible, capped mine shaft. Passing by this shaft, at the next fork go right and head for a stone marker that can be seen on a hill. This is a trig point marker.

Several rare plants may be found in this area, including spring sandwort, which has small brilliant white flowers. From the vantage point by the marker there are views all round, across the Cheshire plain, the Wirral, Lancashire, and south and south-west to the Denbigh moors and the Berwyns: on a clear day, a vista of a vast tract of country.

Curl round the base of the hill with the trig point on it and go left along a track which runs parallel to some electricity lines. This comes out on a stony roadway. Turn right, then left down a wider road. About 200 yards further on, turn right, alongside a wall. This path leads down to another road, just past a sharp bend. Walk uphill to the left, making use of the stony track at the brow of the hill. The route at the start is met with at the T-junction. Turn right and go down the lane, under the bridge and back to the Glan-yr-Afon.

③ Cilcain
The White Horse

Cilcain is a picturesque little village lying to the east of the Clwydian hills in the heart of rural Clwyd. The White Horse is very much part of this scene. It has 14th century origins and is of a similar age to the church of St Mary the Virgin which is just up the road. This ancient pub is a favourite not only with walkers but also with those who enjoy exploring the maze of tranquil and beautiful lanes and by-ways of this part of Clwyd.

Standing down the village street from the church, the White Horse is clearly of considerable age and, in summer especially, is very attractive, with climbing roses around the windows adding to its charm. Inside, the comfortable atmosphere is enhanced by a good selection of beers – it is a freehouse – but Burton's Cask is a special favourite and a good drink after an energetic walk. Other beers available are Ansells, as well as draught Guinness and a range of lagers. For cider drinkers there is Addlestone's draught cider.

The White Horse is open from noon to 3 pm every day and from 7 pm in the evenings. Food is served from 12 noon to 2 pm and from 7.30 pm to 9.30 pm (10 pm on Fridays and Saturdays). During these times there is a wide choice available from sandwiches, ploughman's, home-made curries, ham and eggs, steak and kidney pie to salads. Tables outside allow one to enjoy a meal and the village scene, the front of the White Horse being a sun trap. Only food bought at the pub may be eaten on the premises and children under 14 and well-behaved dogs are permitted inside.

The church of St Mary the Virgin was restored in Victorian times but it is basically 14th century. Outside, one curious feature is that the churchyard is surrounded by a circular wall, specifically so as to leave 'no corners for demons to lurk'. Inside, the very fine carved oak ceiling is quite unexpected in a village church and is well worth seeing. It is thought to have been brought from Basingwerk Abbey, near Flint, when that abbey was dissolved by Henry VIII in 1535. Opposite the church is a house with a large tablet over the door, commemorating the foundation of the village school there in 1799.

Telephone: 01352 740142.

How to get there: Cilcain lies south of the A541 St Asaph/Denbigh to Mold road, signposted to the left about 7 miles out of Mold. Alternatively, it lies northwards of the A494 Mold to Ruthin road, turning off at Tafarn-y-Gelyn.

Parking: There is a car park at the side of the White Horse. It is not very large and certainly a check should be made with the landlord before leaving a car there for a long period. Otherwise parking has to be found elsewhere around the village, there being no public car parks as such.

Length of the walk: 5¼ miles. Map: OS Landranger 116 Denbigh and Colwyn Bay (GR 178653).

This is an energetic walk up to the summit of Moel Fammau and to the Jubilee Tower, but, having gained the summit, the return is all downhill and the struggle is well worth the effort. Moel Fammau at 1,818 ft is the highest point of the Clwydian range of hills. The route runs through open country and provides some good hill walking both uphill and down! There is a long and steep uphill stretch which will need to be taken slowly by even the most active walkers. Sheep will be found everywhere along the whole route and so dogs will need to be kept under tight control most of the way. The walk is suitable for all times of the year, except in frosty conditions, when the uphill stretches may become slippery.

The Walk

From the White Horse go down the lane to the right of the church and follow this lane downhill, then uphill, past a large pond. Above the pond, with a road going off to the left, go straight across this junction,

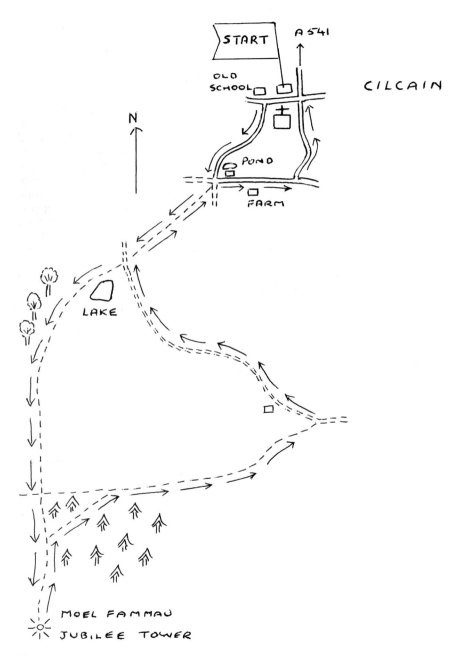

START

A 541

OLD SCHOOL

CILCAIN

POND

FARM

N

LAKE

MOEL FAMMAU
JUBILEE TOWER

through a gateway, then over a stone stile immediately on the right. The path follows the hedge and, a couple of stiles further on, comes to a rough surfaced lane. Go straight across and over another stile. A trout-fishing lake will be seen on the left and then a gate is reached. There is a fine avenue of chestnuts here and, in the summer, redstarts can be seen.

After crossing a stream and going through another gate, the path starts to climb very steeply. This is a well-used path and the constant usage has eroded it in places, so energy, some care, and well-soled footwear are needed on this section. The path winds up the hillside and, towards the brow of this first part, a bridleway runs across at right angles. The route goes straight over, past a wood of conifers, and, being relatively level, one can prepare for the next ascent. The final part up to the Jubilee Tower is another steep climb. At the tower it is worth having a map to identify all the distant landmarks that can be seen in every direction. The Jubilee Tower was built in 1820 to celebrate the diamond jubilee of George III in 1820. In fact, he died the same year. It is a matter of amazement how the massive stone blocks were brought here in the days before JCBs and cranes. The original tower was blown down shortly after being erected, but the massive stone base still remains and is used as a sighting platform, with viewing plaques set into the walls.

On the return, retrace the route back to the wood. About halfway down its length, a simple stile will be seen, with a path running diagonally to the right downhill through the trees. Part of the wood has been cleared but, by keeping straight on across any clearing, a stile will be found at the far side of this wood which crosses its perimeter fence. On the other side the bridleway met with earlier passes along the edge of the wood. Turn right and follow the bridleway downhill. This is pleasant, easy walking on grass and with all the valley spread out below.

Coming into the valley, there is a meeting of ways on the far side of a stile. Turn left and follow the bridleway past a house and through a couple of gates. This rough way eventually meets with the stony lane, crossed over on the way out. Take the path on the right and return to the pond. At this point, take the road to the right, passing Pentre Farm. At the next junction, turn left over a stream and then go up the hill into Cilcain.

Maeshafn
The Miner's Arms

The Miner's Arms is tucked away down a short lane off the green at Maeshafn – a village in itself well away from the main thoroughfares – the Miner's Arms relies on its good name for attracting business. For such a hidden away place to be so well patronised must be an excellent recommendation for the hospitality on offer.

In earlier times the whole area was very much connected with lead mining and the Miner's Arms was the place where local miners gathered each week to receive their weekly pay, no doubt spending some of it before going home! From the outside the pub still has a workmanlike look, stone built and rugged; inside, whilst it retains the old features of stone and wooden beams, there is nothing rugged. It is a very sociable pub with a small, friendly bar, a live fire in the colder months, and a general air of relaxed enjoyment.

Theakston Best Bitter, Courage Directors and Old Peculier all have their adherents and for cider connoisseurs Symond's Scrumpy Jack is on tap.

Meals are available, either in the restaurant, off the bar, or as bar meals. The menu is very comprehensive and includes such dishes as whitebait, egg mayonnaise or soup as starters, while main courses cover both traditional and foreign items. Plaice, gammon, Miner's Arms mixed grill are all available as well as lasagne and chilli con carne. Vegetarians are not forgotten, and all meals are reasonably priced. Sandwiches and ploughman's lunches can also be ordered. There is an equally good selection of desserts. Bar meals are served from 12 noon to 1.45 pm every day and there is a full à la carte menu available from 7 pm to 9 pm on Thursday, Friday and Saturday evenings. Prior booking is recommended. A traditional lunch is served on Sunday. Outside there are tables and you may eat your own food there, providing a drink is bought.

Dogs are not allowed inside the pub, or muddy boots! Being in such a popular walking area, too much mud has been left inside in the past and now a notice has had to be put up banishing dirty boots indoors.

Telephone: 01352 810464.

How to get there: Maeshafn lies south of the A494 Mold to Ruthin road: turn off at either Cadole or Gwernmynydd on to the narrow roads signposted Maeshafn (1¼ miles from the Cadole turning). The Miner's Arms is signposted at the green at Maeshafn, and is only 50 yards down the lane.

Parking: There is ample parking at the pub otherwise park at the green and walk the short way down the lane. As the pub can get busy, it is suggested that, if you leave the car for any length of time, it would be better to park at the green.

Length of the walk: 3 miles. Maps: OS Landranger 117 Chester, and 116 Denbigh and Colwyn Bay (GR 202609).

This is an easy walk, with only one very brief, but steep, uphill section. It is suitable for all seasons, although it can be muddy in places. Dogs can roam freely in the woods and there is only one part where sheep may be grazing. The whole area around Maeshafn is very popular with walkers. The route chosen goes through deciduous woodland and, as such, is different to most others in this book. Public access to woodland of this type is quite rare in North Wales and this walk gives the chance to enjoy such a rarity. Loggerheads country park, which is close by, was set up to help preserve this type of country, especially since, as is so often the case, the flora in this old lead mining and limestone area can be quite special. The woods themselves attract a very wide variety of woodland birds.

The Walk

From the Miner's Arms go right along the track. Turn sharp right at the footpath sign, and go through a small compound of private garages. Up some steps, the path runs along beside a fence, then turns left up

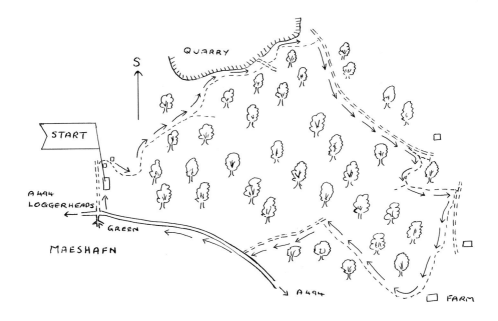

into the beechwood, heading southwards. At a divide in the path, take the left-hand fork. This continues through the wood and, eventually, leads past the edge of a huge quarry.

Quarrying has taken over from lead mining as one of the major industries of the area and although at times it can be noisy on this part of the walk, it is impressive to see the scale of operation. Strangely, wildlife does not seem to be too worried by the noise and jays, nuthatches and woodpeckers can all be seen nearby regularly. The great demand for stone, however, can cause conflict in that quarries are always needing to extend and eat into the countryside, unfortunately, often in those very areas where there are rare plants needing to be conserved.

A series of steps takes the path downhill into a valley. Cross the roadway and take the path opposite which descends down another series of steps away from the quarry. Cross a small meadow which in summer is a place for orchids and join a stony access road. Turn right and walk down through the woods until, eventually, a house is seen ahead. Leave the roadway here and take the path to the right. Just before a wooden field gate, go to the right on a path which climbs steeply up the side of a wooded hill. At the brow, take the left-hand path which runs downhill through the wood. This leads to a field gate and stile. Across the fence, turn right up the cart track, then, after only a few yards, follow the path which runs close to the fence on the right.

An old cottage will be seen in a meadow on the left and it is here that sheep may be found grazing. Further along the fence, there is a stile which takes the path back into the wood. Follow the fence along the edge of the wood on the inside and, when a farm is seen ahead, stay in the wood and bear to the right, uphill. This path joins a cart track which can be very muddy, especially if there has been some tree clearance taking place. Bearing to the left, follow the cart track, a gate on to a lane is reached. Turn right and walk back to Maeshafn and the Miner's Arms.

Llanarmon-yn-Ial
The Raven Inn

The Raven was certainly in existence in 1722 as this is the date that can be clearly seen on the gable end, but whether it was ever involved in the village's older claim to fame is not known. The eldest daughter of George Lloyd, Bishop of Chester from 1604 to 1615, married Thomas Yale from the village and their grandson, Elihu Yale (1648 to 1721), was the founder of the famous American university of that name in New Haven, Connecticut. Certainly it seems as if this small, neat village has something special about it. Set around the large, tree-lined churchyard, with the little church of St Garmon in the middle, the stone-built, terraced cottages and houses that face the church make Llanarmon a pleasing place to visit.

A calm air pervades the village, and there is a strong feeling of space and that the hurly-burly of modern traffic and the world of changing values is far away. The Raven adds to this image as it has a very pleasing frontage in the style of a country building of the early 18th century. Set back from the road that runs around the churchyard and facing south, with its entrance through an archway covered by a Russian vine, it positively invites you to go in. The garden itself is full of colour in the spring and summer and in one area plenty of tables are provided to allow enjoyment of the village scene as well as what the Raven has to offer.

Inside, visitors are sure of a welcome. There is a central bar in one large room with open fires at both ends of the room. The low beams and polished wood add to the old world atmosphere. A fire is lit in the bar when the weather gets colder and it is a very convivial place in which to enjoy a drink: modern heating never seems to be able to match the cheer of a real fire. Tetley, Flowers and Boddington Cream are served. Cider drinkers are catered for with Scrumpy Jack on draught, Beamish Stout, and a guest ale which is changed each week.

Bar meals are varied and are served from 12 noon to 2 pm. There is a full Sunday lunch. Children are welcome and the Raven also provides bed and breakfast.

Opening times are Sunday to Thursday 12 noon to 4 pm and 7 pm to 11 pm. Friday and Saturday 12 noon to 11 pm. There is a full restaurant menu daily 7 pm to 11 pm.

Telephone: 01824 780787.

How to get there: Llanarmon-yn-Ial lies on the B5431, ¼ mile from its junction with the B5430, 10 miles north-west of Wrexham. It is about 6 miles south-east of Ruthin. From the A494 Ruthin to Mold road the village is signposted, to the south, between Llanbedr-Dyffryn-Clwyd and Loggerheads.

Parking: There is parking close to the Raven and elsewhere in the village. Please ask permission before parking all day.

Length of the walk: 3½ miles, with an additional 2 miles for those feeling energetic. Map: OS Landranger 116 Denbigh and Colwyn Bay (GR 191563).

This is an easy walk with only one really steep, but short, uphill section. There is a brief walk through thick bracken and undergrowth in the summer and bare legs should be avoided! On the upland parts of the route there is no cover and weatherproof gear should be used. About half the route is through sheep-grazing land, so dogs will need to be kept well in control. This walk provides a varied mixture of farmland and hill country, and is a good one for all seasons. One part goes along Offa's Dyke path, as it traverses the hills. There are good views of the Vale of Clwyd and of the country towards the Dee and Chester.

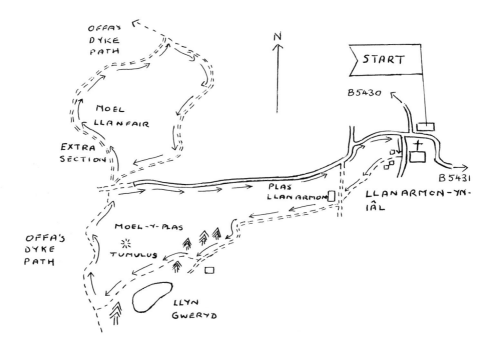

The Walk

Leaving the Raven, turn right and go around the low, western wall of the churchyard. Halfway down this wall, on the opposite side of the road, there is a stone stile. Climb over, go past a garage, and then go through a gate. This leads into a small estate of new houses. Bearing right through the estate, at the far end, there is a stile, with a second stile shortly afterwards. Following the line of a tall hedge, two further stiles are crossed and, over the last stile, a farm will be seen straight ahead. Cross the field in a direct line to a mound with a marker pole on it. On the far side of this mound, the path meets with a cart track, close to Plas Llanarmon, a large farmhouse.

A stony track leads straight past Plas Llanarmon across open countryside. At the end of a wood, the track bears to the left and curves around the wood. A house on the left is reached and, just past this house, on the right, there is a stile and a path which goes up through a belt of trees. On the far side, turn left and continue along beside the trees. There is a lake on the left, Llyn Gweryd, used for fishing and with a large collection of water birds on it – geese, ducks and coots. Initially, keep parallel with the shore of the lake, then with the edge of a further belt of trees.

In summer, this part may be quite overgrown with bracken and undergrowth and the actual path may be hard to follow but persevere and aim for the trees. At the far end of the belt of trees, a simple stile crosses over a wire fence. On the far side, walk to the right, beside the fence, up to a well-built wooden stile. This is where the route joins the Offa's Dyke pathway which runs for 149 miles from South Wales to Prestatyn in the north.

Over the stile, there is a steep climb through open hill pasture, past Moel-y-Plas (1,444 ft) which has an Iron Age tumulus on its summit. Near the brow of the hill, a stile on the left will be seen. Cross over and follow the clearly visible path downhill. This meets up with a cart track in the valley.

For the shorter walk, turn right here and then continue down the metalled lane back to Llanarmon-yn-Ial. A longer route adds about 2 miles to the walk. This is achieved by continuing to follow Offa's Dyke path straight across the cart track and up the hillside, bearing left. This curves round the side of Moel Llanfair, initially uphill, then down, and up again along a track. After a long and fairly steep climb, Offa's Dyke path goes to the left, near to the brow of the hill. At this point do not cross the stile, but go straight on a few yards and through a field gate to the right. A visible trackway leads around the hill, falling away downhill until it returns to that point where the extra walk started. Turn left down the cart track and to the lane. This will come back to Llanarmon-yn-Ial. A stream runs down the valley and it is a pleasant companion on the return to the Raven.

Rhewl
6 The Sun Inn

Set in the hills of the Dee valley, between Corwen and Llangollen, the Sun is a 14th century drovers' inn of great character and atmosphere. Certainly, approaching the Sun down the narrow lanes along the valley, whether from Corwen or Llangollen, the old inn looks its age. Inside, the bar is small and cosy but full of a sense of its past. Dark beams, a glowing fire and polished wood provide just the right mood for a drink after a walk on the hills.

At the other side of the entrance, there is a room with a fine old, black range set into the wide fireplace and here parties can gather, and children are allowed. A piano completes the picture, coming into its own especially at the time of the Llangollen International Musical Eisteddfod, held every year in early July. Then you may hear many languages other than Welsh and English being spoken in the bar, as well as music from the piano. A small snug is an extra hidden-away corner for a sociable drink. The Sun offers Worthington Best, Bass Mild and many guest beers and was awarded CAMRA Pub of the Year in 1997. Murphy's Stout is also to hand for those who prefer a change to Guinness, together with Wrexham lager. An unusually wide selection of malt whiskies is another feature of the Sun.

An outside games room helps to pass the time in all weathers, but, when the sun shines, there is a sheltered and pleasant garden, away from the sound of the traffic, in which to enjoy oneself.

The old drovers' road passed by here, used for moving livestock to the main markets, long before the days of trains and cattle trucks. Many of the drovers, who were an important part of the life of rural communities, were great characters and many books have been written about their exploits and lives. Old photos in the pub give a picture of how life was in earlier days. In the 1820s Thomas Telford built the London to Holyhead road down the far side of the valley, now the A5, leaving Rhewl untouched by modern traffic.

Needless to say, in such a pub, a good, plain menu is offered, at reasonable prices. Sandwiches, salads, jacket potatoes, braised steak, pork, and beef and beer pie are some of what is provided. On Sundays there is always a roast lunch.

Dogs are allowed indoors, although a Great Dane might fill up the bar! Opening times are noon to 11 pm every day, and on Saturday and Sunday from 12 noon to 10.30 pm.

Telephone: 01978 861043.

How to get there: On the A542 Llangollen to Ruthin road, 1½ miles from the bridge at Llangollen, turn left on to the B5103, marked Corwen, Llantysilio and Rhewl. Rhewl is 2 miles down this road. Alternatively, on the A5 turn northwards at Glyndyfrdwy across the Dee, and then turn right for Rhewl. The Sun lies in the fork of two roads. The B5103 is a very narrow and winding road and care should be taken.

Parking: There is a good-sized car park in front of the Sun.

Length of the walk: 3¾ miles. Maps: OS Landranger 125 Bala and Lake Vyrnwy, and 116 Denbigh and Colwyn Bay (GR 176447).

A walk up Llantysilio mountain, through oakwoods initially, then across the open hillside and back through woods again. This is beautiful and unspoilt country, close to the Horseshoe Pass, and, if taken steadily, will generate a thirst! There is plenty of bird-life to be seen: woodpeckers and sparrow-hawks in the oakwoods, amongst others, and, in the open, whinchats, ravens, buzzards and, very rarely, on the tops, merlins. Redpolls and siskins inhabit the coniferous woods on the return. There is a long, steep climb during the first part of the walk, then it is downhill all the way back. After heavy rain, some parts can be slippery and good soled footwear is advised. More than half the route is through open sheep-grazing country.

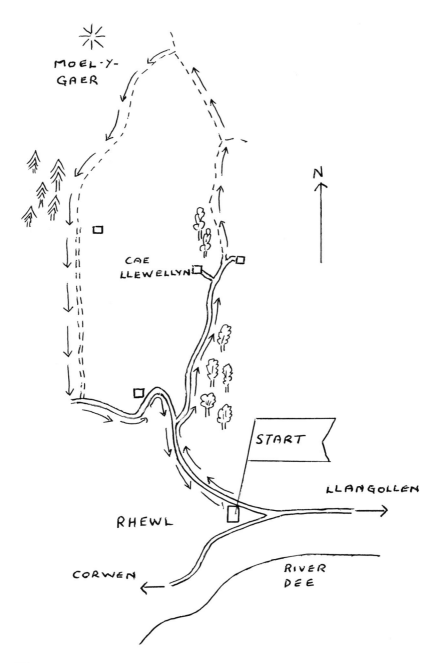

MOEL-Y-GAER

N

CAE LLEWELLYN

START

LLANGOLLEN

RHEWL

CORWEN

RIVER DEE

The Walk

From the Sun, take the lane signposted to Cymmo, along the side of the valley, and, where this lane forks, take the right-hand fork, marked Cae Llewellyn. This is a long, steep climb through the woods. At the entrance to Cae Llewellyn, carry on uphill along a stony cart track, past Ty'n-y-Mynydd on the right. Still climbing, go through a gate on to the mountain, the path running alongside a wood and carry on beside this wood. The path joins up with a track coming around the side of the hill. This next section can be very slippery in wet weather, so take care. Cross over another old gate with a makeshift stile and keep alongside the fence. At that point where the fence drops away downhill, keep straight on, more or less level. After 50–100 yards, bear left up the side of the hill, ignoring a path which runs to the right up into a cwm. In high summer this part can be overgrown with bracken, but the way through will be obvious. After a long, steady climb up the hillside, a stile is reached, close to the brow of the hill, bear left, after about 200–300 yards, another stile will be seen to the left. Moel-y-Gaer (1,654 ft) is close by. The views are magnificent from here of the wooded valley of the Dee and of the Berwyn mountains. This part of the route is not more than a mile from the Horseshoe Pass, due east.

Crossing the stile, follow the path downhill, initially over rocky ground, then, in summer, through thick bracken. The path is clearly visible, even if the fronds tend to grow over it and are almost head high. Towards the bottom of the hill, the path bears right through a gate and passes along the edge of a coniferous wood. It develops into a cart track, passing Bwlch-y-Garnedd on the left, and, eventually, meets with a lane. Turn left here, passing Acer Ddu, and crossing a small river. The lane then rejoins the earlier part of the route. Turn right and walk back to the Sun.

7 Llangollen
The Sun Trevor

About 2 miles east of Llangollen, the Sun Trevor is in a prominent position on the main Llangollen to Ruabon and Wrexham road. It looks out from its vantage point across the Vale of Llangollen, and the Llangollen Canal, as well as the Llangollen golf course, and so provides its customers with a panorama that is full of a variety of interests.

In the past, the Sun Trevor was a substantial farmhouse, parts dating back to the 16th century, and some of the solid, stone barns and outhouses still remain.

Being in such a fine location, close to the main road, the canal, and within a short distance of the town, it is a popular and lively place, not only for those driving out, but also for walkers and canal users. Certainly, enjoying a drink in one of the large window bays and looking out over the vale is very satisfying, although there are plenty of other comfortable places in the large bar, close by the fire, or there is the chance to make use of the dining-room which also overlooks the vale.

At the time of the International Musical Eistedfodd, in July, the bar can have a cosmopolitan atmosphere.

The Sun Trevor is also popular for its choice of draught beers,

32

Webster's Yorkshire Bitter and Courage Directors bitter, and for those whose taste is for stout, Beamish and Guinness. Strongbow is provided for cider drinkers.

For such a prominent pub, meals will always be in demand. At night there is a full restaurant service in the dining-room and a wide selection of bar meals. Meals are also available at lunchtime, in the dining room. The menu ranges from simple fare such as sandwiches and ploughman's to salads and basket meals, home-made steak and kidney pie, breast of chicken or gammon steak, amongst other items. Vegetarians and children are also well catered for.

The Sun Trevor is open every day from 11 am to 3 pm and from 6.30 pm to 11 pm, except Sundays, when the opening time is at noon and 6.30 pm. Although the bar opens at 11 am, coffee is served from 10 am onwards.

Dogs are not allowed indoors and muddy boots are definitely banned!

Telephone: 01978 860651/860312.

How to get there: The Sun Trevor lies on the A539 Llangollen to Ruabon and Wrexham road, 1¾ miles from the bridge at Llangollen. It is very prominent and easy to find.

Parking: There is a large car park in front and at the side of the pub.

Length of the walk: 4½ miles. Map: OS Landranger 117 Chester (GR 244425).

No book concerned with walking in North Wales could leave out at least one route around Llangollen. There is so much of interest in the area as well as some excellent walks, and this one is suitable for all times of the year.

At the start there is a steady climb and a steep ascent to Dinas Bran, which is well worth the effort. At the summit are the historic ruins, views of Llangollen and the vale and the hills beyond, as well as the chance to see the remains of Valle Crucis Abbey, about 1½ miles north-west. This Cistercian abbey was founded in 1201 and dissolved in the 1530s by Henry VIII. It was one of the country's major abbeys during the Middle Ages.

Returning through the edge of the town allows you to see the terminus of the Llangollen steam railway, which uses some of the old Great Western locomotives to haul the trains.

At least half the route is through unfenced sheep farming country, with many sheep roaming about, with the final stages along the canal towpath.

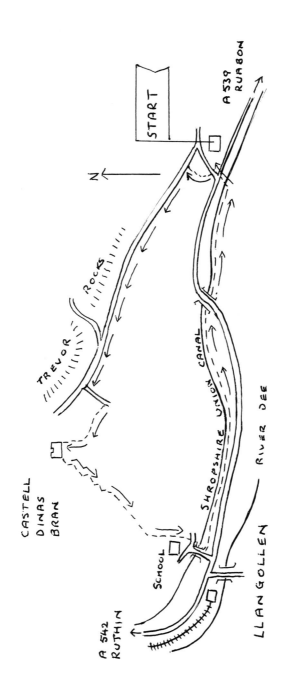

START

N

A 539
RUABON

ROCKS

TREVOR

SHROPSHIRE UNION CANAL

RIVER DEE

CASTELL
DINAS
BRAN

SCHOOL

LLANGOLLEN

A 542
RUTHIN

The Walk

A few yards up the lane that runs beside the Sun Trevor, a signposted path will be seen on the left. This path is a steep one and eventually comes out on another road. Turn left and walk along this single-track road uphill, through a variety of country and at the base of the cliffs, Creigiau Eglwyseg. These woods are a good place to see nuthatches, treecreepers, and woodpeckers, as well as redstarts and pied fly-catchers in the summer. After about 1¼ miles, a road to the right branches off and, shortly afterwards, a lane to the left, with a cattle grid, is reached. Turn down here and within 100 yards there is a stile on the right which leads into a meadow. Follow the path across this meadow and up the very steep ascent to Dinas Bran. The ruins on the summit can be clearly seen, even if it takes some energy to get to them! This site was an Iron Age hill fort, then a wooden castle in the 13th century, with stone fortifications added later. The stone castle only lasted for a short period, as by the late 1500s it was a ruin.

It is worth spending a short time on the summit and enjoying the widespread views. On the far side of Dinas Bran, take the zigzag path downhill to the end of a wooded lane. This goes down into Llangollen, close by the school. At the canal, cross to the lower side and walk along the towpath to the left. There is a small exhibition here about canals and narrow boats; also the Llangollen railway has its terminus nearby and there is a chance to have a look at the steam engines and other railway memorabilia.

The 1½ mile walk back to the Sun Trevor is all alongside the canal and is a part of the route that is always a pleasure to walk along, whether for just being by the water, or looking at the narrow boats, or the fish or at a kingfisher trying to catch one. The towpath passes under the A539 and, at the next stone bridge, cross over and return to the Sun Trevor, just across the road.

⑧ Llangynhafal
The Golden Lion

The rural nature of the countryside around Llangynhafal is reflected in the Golden Lion, a charming 17th century pub that still retains a feeling of being closely connected with the country and the local farming community. In the old days, and within living memory of a very few, the publican farmed about 100 acres and his wife dispensed beer out of jugs on the bar to thirsty farmworkers and any passing travellers. Nowadays that way of life has long gone and the Golden Lion provides hospitality to a much wider clientele.

The many old photos on the walls of the lounge, together with some memories of the days of horse power, create a warm and intimate feeling of being a guest of the landlord and part of this small farming community. Pewter tankards hanging over the bar are a further reminder of the days when each regular had his own tankard and, as soon as he came in, the landlord took it down and filled it without being asked.

Another of the features of the Golden Lion is the beautiful Virginia creeper outside, which grows in profusion across the front of the pub in spring and summer and into the autumn. Seats outside provide a good spot for walkers, down from the hills, to relax and enjoy a good drink. Tetley Bitter and a guest bitter are always available. The guest varies from Benskins to the local Denbigh bitter – a dark ale – and others. Ansells Mild is also there and lager. Draught Guinness is provided for those whose taste is for something heavier, and Scrumpy Jack should satisfy cider drinkers.

The 26 seat dining-room is off the lounge bar and provides a place on Saturday nights for a good singsong. The pub's music maker has been playing at these popular sessions for around 25 years! Children are welcome in the lounge, but not dogs. They can join their owners in the bar. The menu reflects the retention of older traditions, especially the desserts offered – old favourites such as spotted dick, apple pie, fruit crumble and treacle sponge are all there, as well as others. The main course also includes firm favourites such as steak and kidney pie, gammon and rump steak. For those wanting something lighter, bar meals are available – sandwiches, ploughman's, toasted sandwiches, bacon and egg, or salad, besides all those meals children enjoy.

The Golden Lion opens from noon to 3 pm every day, except Wednesdays, and in the evening from 7 pm to 11 pm every day.

Telephone: 01824 790451.

How to get there: Llangynhafal lies to the east of the B5429 Bodfari to Llanbedr-Dyffryn-Clwyd road, with several lanes being clearly signposted to it. The approach is down narrow country lanes.

Parking: There is a large car park at the rear of the pub, and cars can be left whilst on a walk.

Length of the walk: 2½ or 6¼ miles. The route lends itself to two approaches. One for those who are more leisurely inclined and who are looking for a rural walk through lanes and up a bridleway, steep at the top, with historic interest on the way, or the other which is an addition to the shorter walk and provides an exhilarating and energetic hike across the top of the Clwydian hills. Map: OS Landranger 116 Denbigh and Colwyn Bay (GR 129635).

Both the short and long routes go down country lanes to the little village of Gellifor, before climbing into the hills along a bridlepath, passing a likely badger's set on the way. The shorter walk then returns downhill past the old house where Wordsworth sometimes came to stay and past the little church of St Cynhafal (the key is kept at the farm opposite). The longer walk continues into the higher hills and follows Offa's Dyke pathway across the tops, with an exhilarating series of views of hills and valleys.

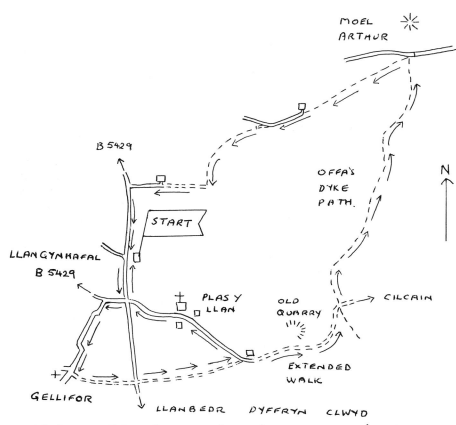

The longer walk has a few steep sections and covers some exposed country over the hills, and the shorter walk has one steep climb, but both are suitable at all times of the year. Some stretches of the walks are free of sheep.

The Walk

Setting out from the Golden Lion go left down the lane, and at the crossroads turn right, then, shortly afterwards, left to Gellifor.

On entering the village, past Gellifor Farm, go left, and opposite the large 1860 chapel, take the lane on the left which leads to a bridleway. This passes a renovated barn and goes alongside a stream. It rises steadily uphill, crosses a lane and continues upwards. Oak, holly and cherry trees line the bridleway and the banks have some large holes in them, almost certainly dug by badgers. As the way gets steeper, it also gets muddier. Near the top, just beyond a small pond on the right, a gate is reached.

Beyond it, close to some electricity lines, there is another gate, and through here the path joins with a lane.

For the shorter walk, turn left, downhill. For the longer walk, turn right, uphill.

Taking the shorter walk first, the lane runs downhill between high banks, eventually reaching Plas y Llan, an old house which has been carefully modernised. This house is where the poet William Wordsworth stayed in 1791 and 1793, on the latter visit having walked all the way from the Isle of Wight! He was a college friend of the son of the house, Robert Jones, and they had been on a walking tour of Europe together in 1790. Just below Plas y Llan is the little church of St Cynhafal, which has, in the unlocked porch, a history of the building as well as of Plas y Llan. The key for the church itself is with the house opposite. Continuing down the lane, turn right at the crossroads at the bottom and head back to the Golden Lion.

For the longer walk, continue up the lane, past Dol-y-Caeau. This lane comes out on to open hill country and turns into a cart track which winds its way up into the hills, passing a small, disused quarry on the left. The track rises steeply through the heather and then reaches a meeting of the ways. A signpost points the way to Cilcain, Moel Fammau and Moel Llys-y-Coed. Take the left-hand path to Moel Llys-y-Coed, up a short but steep hill. This is part of the Offa's Dyke pathway and provides a walk across the tops of the hills that cannot fail to exhilarate all those who enjoy hill walking, with the rounded, rolling hills of Clwyd stretching into the distance, heather covered and open, and with the Vale of Clwyd far below. The path is well laid but there is no cover and the wind is always blowing, so be prepared.

After curving to the right, the path comes to a steep descent. Through usage and wind and rain the way has become eroded and, in wet weather, can be very slippery, so care is needed. At the bottom of the hill, with the high hill of Moel Arthur opposite, there is a lane and cattle grid. Do not go on to this lane, but take the cart track to the left, immediately before coming to the lane. This cart track goes downhill, passing Siglen Uchaf on the right. A gate leads on to a narrow lane. Ahead there is a straight stretch and then this lane bears to the right, past a clump of trees. Just before this bend, take the cart track on the left which leads up to a field gate.

Beyond this gate, the track keeps close to a wall and hedge, bearing around to the left. Eventually, a gateway on the right is reached which is at the head of a cart track coming up the hill from the right. Go down this cart track, which can be muddy, past the entrance to Pentre Farm on the right, and then on to a T-junction. The lane to the left leads back to the Golden Lion.

9 Llanrhaeadr
The King's Head Inn

It is not hard to understand why the King's Head is such a popular pub, being close to the busy main road from Denbigh to Ruthin but not disturbed by it, in a beautiful setting, and providing the most comprehensive hospitality. It is open all day and every day for meals and a drink in comfortable surroundings.

There are two bars. One, presided over by wooden carvings of a witch and a warlock, provides a setting in keeping with the age of the pub. The other, in a converted steading, has a more modern flavour, looking out over the Vale of Clwyd. Cacti line the window sills and the whole is reminiscent of holidays on the Continent and sunnier climes. Both bars, however, serve Bass Bitter, Bass Mild, Worthington Best Bitter and a selection of lagers, as well as draught Guinness and Red Rock cider.

In conjunction with the beer on offer, part of the popularity of the pub must also lie with the choice of food provided. The menu lists 93 items and, whilst it would be impossible to note all the possibilities, there are, in addition to starters such as French onion soup with cheese croûtons, fish, poultry and mixed grills, omelettes, pasta dishes, sandwiches and snacks like baked beans on toast – in fact, something to suit everyone's taste and appetite, not forgetting the children. This extensive menu is available all day up to 10 pm.

The King's Head is a 16th century inn which once stood beside the ford across the stream that now flows down beside the car park. In those days the stream must have been much larger. Later, a bridge was built to take the main road over the ford and this meant that part of the King's Head dropped below road level, as can be seen. Later still, with increasing traffic, a bypass was built and this has left the village and pub more peaceful. It is now a haven to relax in, or stay at, as there are letting bedrooms available for bed and breakfast.

Without the hustle of heavy traffic, the village has regained its charm. Directly opposite the pub is the church of St Dyfnog, the early 18th century almshouses, and the old smithy, now a pottery. The church, of 6th century origin, is in itself of special interest. St Dyfnog chose this site because of the well nearby, whose waters were thought to have great healing powers. The church has a squat 13th century tower and a 15th century double-aisled nave, a style common in this part of Clwyd. It is the glass and woodwork that are outstanding in such a country church. The Jesse window, depicting the lineage of Jesus from the royal house of David, whose father was Jesse, is of national fame. It was installed in 1533, and during the civil war of 1642 was hidden away to prevent it being smashed by the Puritans. In 1661, following the restoration of Charles II to the throne, it was restored. In 1940 it was protected again, this time because of fears about damage from air raids. The glass at the other end of the church, although older, was not so lucky and was smashed by the Puritans. The broken pieces were carefully restored and reset 200 years later in the 1840s.

The timber and carvings in the barrel roof of the nave and in the lych-gate are also exceptional. At the far end of the churchyard, the 1729 almshouses add a picturesque touch.

Telephone: 01745 890278.

How to get there: Llanrhaeadr lies to the west of the A525 Denbigh to Ruthin road. The village is now bypassed but the turnings off along the new road are clearly signposted. The King's Head is directly opposite the church.

Parking: There is a large car park at the side of the pub.

Length of the walk: 3 miles. Map: OS Landranger 116 Denbigh and Colwyn Bay (GR 082634).

A not too taxing walk which is suitable for all weathers although there are one or two muddy parts in wet weather.

41

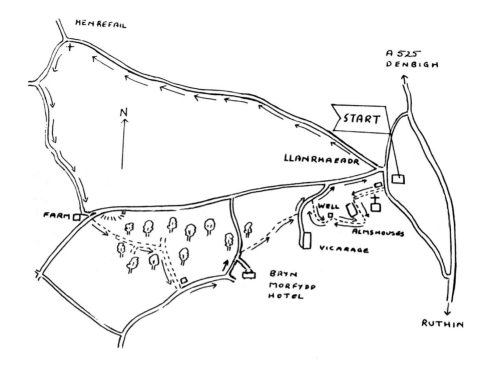

The route shows off this part of rural Clwyd to its best: winding, sunken lanes and woods, with far distant views across the fertile fields of the old town of Denbigh and its castle on the hill, and also of a rural landscape of villages and square church towers set against a backdrop of the Clwydian hills. For golfing enthusiasts, part of the route runs through the middle of the Bryn Morfydd golf course, a local example of the latest trend in farmland diversification.

The Walk

From the King's Head, cross the road to the old smithy which is now the Anvil Pottery. Walk up the roadway, and just before the almshouses, go through the gateway and cross the top of the churchyard. At the far side there is an archway and the path enters a wood, close to a stream. Follow the path up through the woods, as it crosses and recrosses the stream. St Dyfnog's Well is further up and the bath in which bathers hoped to be cured by the healing waters is still there, even if it has had some modern maintenance work done on it. People must have been much tougher in earlier times to bathe in such water or was the weather warmer?

Beyond the bath, the path bears left, upwards, to a gap in a wall.

42

This leads into a corner of the vicarage garden. Turn right, go through a gateway to the vicarage driveway; turn right again and then, a short distance further on, go through the vicarage entrance gates to a lane. Turn right and walk downhill to a junction. Take the turning on the left and walk uphill, passing some houses. From here there are some fine views of the Clwydian hills to the right. At the top of the hill, the lane narrows and winds its way through pleasant countryside. Denbigh and its castle on top of a prominent hill come into view across the fields.

Generally, there is very little traffic on this lane, apart from farm vehicles and horses. Further on, the hamlet of Hen Refail (Old Smithy) is reached. Turn left up the narrow lane, signposted 'Prion $1\frac{1}{2}$', passing the chapel. After $\frac{1}{4}$ mile the lane forks. Take the left-hand fork, signposted 'Pentre Llanrhaeadr $1\frac{1}{4}$'. This lane goes uphill steadily, passing a small farm on the left and eventually Craig Lwyd Farm is reached on the right side of a sharp left-hand bend. At the triangular green, cross the road to the stile and footpath signpost. Over this stile, for a very short distance, the ground can be extremely muddy, churned up by cattle in wet weather, but by careful hopping from tussock to tussock it can be safely negotiated. Follow the course of the hedge which runs along the top of a small quarry and, at the edge of the wood, a simple stile will be seen.

In the wood, there is a wide track that goes straight ahead and then joins another. Turn left here and follow yellow way marker signs to the edge of the wood. This wood is used for pheasant rearing and, although the route is a public path, dogs should be restrained from harassing the pheasants. On leaving the wood, the track crosses part of a golf course, and leads to a lane near to some farm buildings. Turn left, downhill, keeping left at the next junction. This lane crosses the golf course and, at the bottom of the hill, meets with the main entrance to the Bryn Morfydd hotel. Bear left here and, after about 100–200 yards along this lane, a track to the left runs up towards the course and a gate. A few yards further along from this track on the left, some stone steps will be seen on the right, leading down through the wood. Follow this path along the edge of the wood until a stile at the top of a meadow is reached.

Across the meadow, on the far, lower side, a gate will be seen. Walk along the hedgeside to this gate and rejoin the driveway to the vicarage. Turn left and, after about 100 yards, turn right through the same gateway into the vicarage garden that was used before. Turn down the gap in the wall and follow the path back to the King's Head.

10 Llannefydd
The Hawk and Buckle

Llannefydd, high in the hills to the north-west of Denbigh, is a small, unspoilt village, with those five essential ingredients needed to keep it alive – school, church, pub, shop and village hall. From here there are some fine, panoramic views across the Vale of Clwyd to the east, and to the sea and coastal resorts of Rhyl and Prestatyn. On clear days, even the hills of Cumbria can be seen, almost 100 miles northwards. At one time, Llannefydd was on the main coach route from Denbigh, and the south and east, to Conwy and Holyhead. These were the days when the coastal region was undeveloped and the low lying ground avoided by travellers. Now the old coach road is a quiet country lane and the village is peaceful, undisturbed by modern traffic problems.

Nowadays the Hawk and Buckle can hardly be said to be on the beaten track, and yet it has a fine reputation for good food and hospitality. It is no surprise, therefore, to walk into the pub, which, from its simple exterior, would seem to be a pleasant and unassuming country inn, and find a different world. The spacious and comfortable lounge bar has a warm and welcoming feel about it and, in winter time, a log fire burns brightly. There is also a cheerful and attractive dining-room. On the other side of the entrance to this stone-built 17th century inn, there is a smaller bar with a pool table.

The Hawk and Buckle is a freehouse with an extension at the back to provide ten very well furnished en suite bedrooms which do not spoil the simple, yet attractive frontage of the building. As might be expected the rooms are sought after by those seeking a rural retreat in surroundings that provide such excellent hospitality.

The beers served are Worthington Best Bitter, Caffrey's, Guinness and a couple of lagers. For cider, Taunton Autumn Gold is provided.

The menus are varied, ranging from a wide choice of bar snacks and meals in the pub, together with a good selection of vegetarian dishes, to an extensive menu in the dining-room. Whatever your order at the bar, whether home-made soup with hot roll and butter, or a toasted sandwich, or beef bourguignonne, it is sure to be excellent. Welsh lamb chops, local smoked trout and river caught salmon are samples of the local produce on offer.

Opening times vary between summer and winter. From May to September, the Hawk and Buckle is open from noon to 2 pm every day, but from October to April, it is closed at lunchtime on Monday, Tuesday, Thursday, and Friday. In the evenings, it is open every day from 7 pm to 11 pm (10.30 pm on Sundays).

Across the road is the church of St Nefydd and St Mary. The key to its massive door is kept at the Hawk and Buckle and is on a similar scale to the door. No chance of taking it home accidentally! The church, like many others in the district, is double-aisled, which makes it very large, spacious and light inside.

Telephone: 01745 540249.

How to get there: Llannefydd lies to the north-west of Denbigh and south-east of Abergele, about halfway between the two, down narrow, winding country lanes. From Denbigh take the B5382 road to Henllan and, once there, by the old church tower, take the lane signposted 'Llannefydd'. From Abergele, take the A548 road to Llanrwst and ¾ mile before Llanfair Talhaiarn (the village will be seen ahead in the valley) take the lane on the left, also signposted to 'Llannefydd'. Both routes involve a journey of about 3 miles down the lanes. The Hawk and Buckle is in the middle of the village.

Parking: There is limited parking at the rear of the pub and across the road. A much larger, free, public car park is to be found at the far side of the church, within a minute's walk of the Hawk and Buckle.

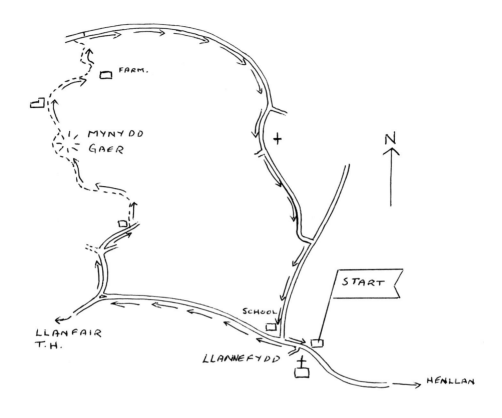

Length of the walk: 3½ miles. Map: OS Landranger 116 Denbigh and Colwyn Bay (GR 983706).

The walk is suitable for all times of the year and, in fact, is well protected along much of the route, apart from the section over Mynydd Gaer. There is usually little traffic along the lanes and there should be no problem for dogs, although sheep do wander freely over Mynydd Gaer.

The view from the top of Mynydd Gaer must be one of the best in Clwyd and looks out over the country in every direction. This Iron Age hill fort, whose outline can still be seen, was a major settlement from around 1,000 BC until the Romans came before AD 100 and time can be spent exploring the site. The lanes leading up to the fort and on the return are full of botanical interest, as are so many in this part of North Wales.

46

The Walk

Starting out from the Hawk and Buckle take the lane heading westwards and walk along it for about ½ mile. This was the old route taken by travellers going to Holyhead and Ireland. At a bend in the road, where there is a triangular junction, turn right up a narrow lane. The hedges here, in season, are full of wild gooseberries which are much prized by local people for jam making and pies.

At the next junction, take the upper lane to the right and immediately, on the far side of a bungalow, turn left along a cart track. This track turns into a grassy path which tends to bear right through the gorse. A wooden gate leads out to the hill, then the path winds up through the gorse, initially bearing to the left, alongside a fence, then branching off diagonally uphill, but still bearing to the left. Follow this path to the summit of Mynydd Gaer, where there are the remains of a 10-acre Iron Age hill fort and settlement. The fort was protected by a defensive ditch around the perimeter of the site with an outer embankment and a massive inner stone wall. Parts of this can still be seen. The entrances to the fort were on the north and south-east parts of the perimeter. The remains of hut circles can also be detected. Nowadays this is a windswept hilltop site, but around 3,000 years ago it was a thriving community. The people then would have looked out over the same distant and magnificent views as now, although the pattern of the countryside would have been different.

Leaving Mynydd Gaer, walk down the grassy track beside a fence. This leads downhill, past the L-shaped smallholding of Ty Newydd. At a meeting of the ways, go right and near to an entrance to a farm, swing left, again downhill, following a zigzag path through the bracken into the bottom of the valley. A single track lane runs along this valley. Turn right along it, and return to Llannefydd, passing on the way the old chapel at Pentre Isaf, dated 1815.

⑪ Llanfair Talhaiarn
The Black Lion

The village of Llanfair Talhaiarn (known locally as Llanfair T.H.) lies beside the river Elwy. During the years from 1874 to 1877, the famous poet-priest Gerard Manley Hopkins lived at nearby St Asaph and spent many days walking in this valley. His sonnet 'In the Valley of the Elwy' lyrically describes his feeling for the countryside close to Llanfair Talhaiarn:

> Lovely the woods, waters, meadows, combes, and vales,
> All the air things wear that build this world of Wales.

It is very likely that he would still recognise the main part of the village, virtually unchanged since his time, although, on the outskirts, modern houses have sprung up.

Within the village, the Black Lion is close to the old bridge over the river Elwy. It is a pub that has old origins but it has been extensively refurbished and redesigned from the days at the turn of the century when old photographs in the bar show it as Byrd's Black Lion Hotel and in a very run-down condition. Robinson's brewery now owns it and it has a reputation as a pub where good meals are served, both in the bar and in the 44-seat restaurant. It is also a base for a good day out in the beautiful valley of the Elwy.

The choice of meals is very large, from bar snacks of jacket potatoes or French bread sandwiches with a wide range of fillings, to bar meals such as chicken breast, scampi, plaice, quiche, pizzas and vegetarian dishes. A fuller à la carte menu is served in the restaurant and every day there are 'specials', such as honey roast duck or pork Normandie, which explains the popularity of the pub.

The Black Lion has two bars: the village bar, with pool table, is where the locals tend to gather and there is also the lounge bar. Both bars serve Robinson's Best Mild and Bitter, as well as draught Guinness and Strongbow cider. A useful addition is draught Wheelwright, low-alcohol beer, which is very well considered and certainly a useful drink for those who are driving.

Children are very welcome in the lounge and have their own menu, but no dogs are allowed indoors. They can join their owners in the beer garden by the river.

The Black Lion is open seven days a week from noon to 3 pm and from 6 pm to 11 pm. Mealtimes are from noon to 2 pm and from 7 pm to 9.30 pm daily. Bed and breakfast is also available.

Telephone: 01745 720205.

How to get there: Llanfair T.H. is on the A548 Abergele to Llanrwst road, about 5 miles south of Abergele. The A548 bypasses the village and to reach the Black Lion, cross the bridge, and the pub is immediately on the left.

Parking: There is ample space beside the pub on most days, except for sunny summer week-ends. There is also a small public car park just across the road.

Length of the walk: 2½ miles. Map: OS Landranger 116 Denbigh and Colwyn Bay (GR 702928).

This is a particularly pleasant all-weather walk along the valley of the Elwy, initially beside the river and then up on the hills to overlook the valley. The return is along another of the flower-rich lanes of Clwyd. There can be few who will not find this walk extremely satisfying.

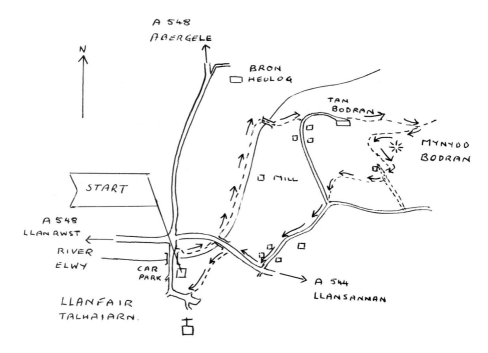

The Walk

From the Black Lion, cross the bridge and turn sharp right at the far side. The path goes beside the river, then over a stile, to the main road. Cross the road and take the path signposted opposite. From here there is a pleasant walk across the fields and beside the Elwy. Along this part there is always the chance of seeing grey wagtails, dippers or a kingfisher. Overlooking the fields is the fine and very large farmhouse, Bron Heulog (Sunny Hill).

At the far end of the fields a footbridge crosses the river. On the other side the path climbs very steeply to a narrow road. There are handrails in places to help climb the hill. At the top, turn left and walk along the road as far as the small farm, Tan Bodran. The road comes to an end here but there is a track which continues uphill past Tan Bodran. At the brow of the hill go through the gate on the right and take the upper path where there is a fork. This upper path keeps on the level for a short way then rises. After about 100 yards, and, after passing two large birch trees, make a U-turn, uphill. The path on the way up can be obscured by bracken in the summer but, with perseverance, it is always to be found.

Nearer the top, walk around the flank of Mynydd Bodran, in an anti-

50

clockwise direction. Do not climb to the summit but, after circling it, some old sheds will be seen ahead. Walk towards them and keep on the upper side of the fence. Close to a house, a stile crosses the fence and gives access on to a road. About 100 yards along this road to the left, a path goes to the right, alongside the remains of an old hedge. Another stile is reached and from here the path runs diagonally down-hill to the left. This is a steep descent, but aim for the far, lower, corner of the field. There is another stile in the corner which brings you to a lane at a junction. Take the sunken lane which goes downhill. It crosses a stream and then goes past the Girl Guide Centre, before entering the outskirts of Llanfair T.H. Past the modern houses and at the main road, turn right downhill and, just around the bend, take the signposted footpath to the left. This comes out in the centre of the village. The Black Lion is to the right out of the little square.

12 Capel Garmon
The White Horse Inn

Capel Garmon is a small, upland village at the upper end of the Conwy valley which looks out westwards towards the rugged peaks of Snowdonia. A compact village, it is quite different in character from those to the east, in Clwyd. The White Horse Inn, with its white walls and black shutters, is the main feature of the village. The little church is now boarded up, although the chapel, at the other end of the village, still holds services and is part of the community, as well as the school, shop and post office, all vital for the survival of small, rural villages. Remote as it is, one of Capel Garmon's claims to fame is the fact that ¾ mile southwards there is an archaeologically famous chambered tomb, a cromlech, which is visited by a large number of people of all nationalities.

The White Horse is a 17th century pub, which has expanded into the cottage next door, and this has been converted into a charming, old world style dining-room, the 'Old Cottage Eating Room'. Upstairs, the White Horse provides bed and breakfast with en suite bedrooms.

The bar area is very much in the old country manner, with several small, cosy rooms that provide an intimate atmosphere, especially coupled with the old dark beams, log fires, shining brass and an interesting collection of teapots and jugs hanging up.

The White Horse is the second pub in this book to sport a ghost (the first being the Blue Lion at Cwm). This time, a blonde woman in a white dress is seen. She has appeared several times in part of the bar area, and elsewhere, and is generally thought of as being friendly but 'mischievous'. Her history does not appear to be commonly known, although most seem to agree that her white dress is something to do with a wedding and that a misfortune occurred at that time of her life. Certainly, there is a welcoming and friendly atmosphere which gives no feeling of any chilly presences.

At this freehouse you may drink Stones Best Bitter, Bass cask ale and Mild, together with Guinness and a selection of lagers.

The inn is open for lunch in the restaurant on Wednesday, Saturday and Sunday, and every evening for bar meals. There is a varied menu and the Sunday lunches are very popular. It has a reputation for good food and hospitality. The restaurant serves a full dinner menu. Children are welcome in the rooms away from the bar, and friendly, well-behaved dogs are allowed in.

Telephone: 01690 710271.

How to get there: Capel Garmon lies 2½ miles to the east of the A470 Llanrwst to Betws-y-Coed road. The turning up a narrow lane is clearly signposted, about halfway between the two towns. The White Horse is in the middle of the village.

Parking: There is a good sized car park at the rear of the pub and cars can be left there by patrons going on a walk, but ask the landlord first.

Length of the walk: 3½ miles. Map: OS Landranger 116 Denbigh and Colwyn Bay (GR 815555).

Tucked away in the hills of the upper Conwy valley, this all-year-round walk demonstrates the sudden change in the character of the countryside from Clwyd into Snowdonia. Gone are the rolling hills and secluded valleys and vales; instead the country is now one of rugged rocks and outcrops with stands of oak. The mountain peaks are closer and even the farms seem to huddle more into the landscape. For those interested in archaeology and pre-history, the nationally famous three-chambered tomb is well worth seeing and the route passes within yards of it.

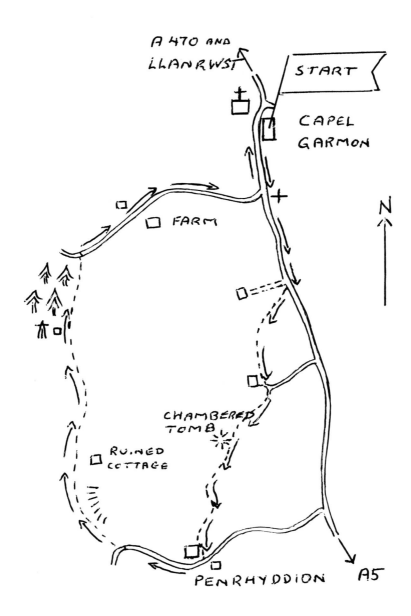

A 470 and
LLANRWST

START

CAPEL
GARMON

N

FARM

CHAMBERED
TOMB

RUINED
COTTAGE

PENRHYDDION

A5

54

The Walk

From the White Horse, take the lane heading southwards, past the chapel. About 100 yards beyond the entrance to the farm, Maes-y-Garnedd, cross the stile on the right. The waymarked path runs alongside a hedge. Passing through a gateway, go straight along a paved path, past a grove of oak trees. At the farm, take the path up the bank and go through the upper gateway, crossing the farmyard of Ty'n-y-Coed, and onto the access road. Signs show the way to the burial chamber, which is in the keeping of the Department of the Environment. The chamber can be visited. It was originally covered by a mound of earth and stones and first excavated in 1853. The outline of the mound is now indicated by a series of small stones, and the western chamber has been used as a stable until recently. It is thought that this tomb was in use around 2000 BC and was for the communal burial of the dead. It is unusual to find such a tomb in North Wales, as its design is more akin to burial chambers found in south-east Wales and the Cotswolds. More information can be obtained from Ty'n-y-Coed Farm.

From the chamber, about 50 yards to the south-west, there is a kissing-gate. Through this gate, the route passes around a knoll and then heads for a footpath sign that will be seen about 100 yards on the far side of a meadow. Another kissing-gate is reached, and, from here, follow the track up a short incline. At the top, another footpath sign will be seen, straight ahead. Bear right, and go down the cart track, through the farmyard of Penrhyddion Ucha.

At the access road, turn right. This roadway runs downhill and through a gate. On the far side of this gate, it takes a sharp turn to the left, but on this bend, go straight ahead and off the road. An old track runs along the base of a small, wooded hill, eventually rising up a hill past a ruined cottage on the right.

The cart track continues alongside a wall, across the hills, passing through several gateways. At the edge of a wood, quite surprisingly in such a remote place, you come across a radio mast and small service building. Carry on along the edge of the wood, downhill, and onto an access road by a gate. Turn right here along the lane and return to Capel Garmon. It is worth noting the old drystone buildings that are to be seen along this lane, indeed the whole area has a very ancient aspect to it.

⑬ Betws-y-Coed
The Miner's Bridge Inn

Standing solidly beside the A5, just to the west of Betws-y-Coed, the Miner's Bridge Inn could not be said to be off the beaten track, as some of the other pubs are in this book. It is less than 20 years since the old Oakfield Hotel was converted to a pub, in fact the only one in the whole of Betws-y-Coed, as all the other establishments are classed as hotels. The Miner's Bridge, however, has carried on the tradition of providing bed and breakfast accommodation throughout the year, with en suite, centrally heated, and double-glazed bedrooms. Part of the pub was also, until quite recently, the local post office and shop for the little community of Pentre Du.

In much older times, the Roman road known as Sarn Helen, which ran southwards from the Roman fort at Caerhun in the Conwy valley, was likely to have crossed the river Llugwy very near to where the Miner's Bridge now stands, and headed across the hills to Dolwyddelan. Later, the footbridge over the Llugwy was used by the lead miners on their way to the mines in what is now Gwydyr Forest. The ruins of many of these mines can still be found throughout the area. Always a popular spot with walkers, the Miner's Bridge Inn is well placed as a centre for many good walks through the forest.

This inn is a freehouse, open all day and every day from noon to 11 pm, apart from a short period in the afternoon. The real ales provided are Bass cask, for those who prefer a stronger drink, and Worthington Best for a lighter tipple. M&B Mild is also available, as well as draught Guinness and a couple of lagers. Cider drinkers have Strongbow cider.

Bar meals are served all day. The menu offers a range from sirloin steak, gammon, chicken, scampi, plaice or quiches to cottage pie, curry, hamburgers, steak and onion sandwiches or lasagne. In the evenings, a special such as beef and Guinness casserole is added to the menu in addition to the normal fare.

Children are welcome and it is a pub which seems to lend itself to providing for families – spacious and comfortable inside, with a very pleasant garden and tables outside. There are three bars: one has a pool table, the others have plenty of room for you to spread out and enjoy the fine views across the Llugwy valley which, in autumn especially, is a colourful mass of russets, red and browns, interspersed with the dark green of the conifers. Dogs have to stay outside but can join their owners in the garden if on a lead.

Telephone: 01690 710386.

How to get there: The Miner's Bridge Inn is on the A5, about ¾ mile westwards from the Pont-y-Pair bridge in the centre of Betws-y-Coed.

Parking: There is a large and accessible car park at the side of the pub. Walkers can leave their cars, if making use of the pub, but they should ask the landlord first.

Length of the walk: 4 miles. Map: OS Landranger 115 Caernarfon and Bangor (GR 779568).

Gwydyr Forest, created in the early 1920s, is an area that has walks to suit everyone, from a stroll by the river to serious, long-distance hikes across the hills. It is not just block upon block of conifers, like many other of the recently planted forests, but has a varied mix of open country, smallholdings, native broad-leaved trees and conifers, which are the main crop. Intermingled with the trees, there is the historical interest of the old lead mines. Several mines are being restored as visitor attractions. The forest is also becoming increasingly colonised by birds typical of coniferous woods, such as crossbills, siskins, redpolls and, in places, goshawks.

The walk is suitable for all seasons. It includes one long and fairly steep section which will create a thirst in the most energetic of walkers. This is a walk where dogs can run freely virtually all the way around the route.

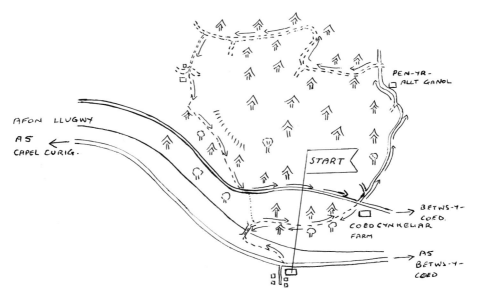

AFON LLUGWY

A5 ← CAPEL CURIG.

PEN-YR-ALLT GANOL

START

BETWS-Y-COED.

COEDCYNHELIAR FARM

A5 BETWS-Y-COED

The Walk

From the pub, cross the main road with care. Diagonally opposite, there is a stone stile in the wall. On the other side, the path runs through the wood, alongside the Llugwy, a river that can be spectacular in full spate or restful and full of deep pools in calmer times. This is the place to see dippers and grey wagtails. Somewhere near this part of the river, there is the location where Sarn Helen forded it, although the exact spot is not now precisely known. Walkers can make their own judgement as to where it was most likely to have been. The woods here are full of beech and sweet chestnut trees, which provide that welcome change from conifers that is such a feature of Gwydir Forest. Go down the steps at the miner's bridge, but take care as they can be very slippery in the wet. Climb up the bridge which crosses the Llugwy at a point where the river rushes down in a torrent. This was the place where the miners crossed the river on their way to the lead mines, many spending the week up in the hills, sleeping in barracks near the mines and returning at the weekends.

At the top of the bridge, bear right, diagonally up the hill, following a clearly defined path through the trees. Initially on the level, it later climbs up to meet a forest lane, close by Coedcynheliar Farm. Take the forest lane opposite which climbs steeply for ¾ mile. There are many streams running down this hillside and also patches of open country and a wide variety of woodland birds may be seen, such as jays, goldcrests, coal tits, siskins, redpolls, buzzards and sometimes crossbills.

After a stiff climb, Pen-yr-Allt Ganol is reached. There is a short stretch on the level, then the lane rises steeply again. A crossroads is reached and here turn left onto a Forestry Commission road. It is important to follow the route instructions carefully from here onwards as the whole forest is criss-crossed by a maze of these roads and once off the route it is easy to become really lost.

At the next Y-junction, go to the right, the road curving around to the left, with the mass of the mountain, Moel Siabod, appearing directly ahead. At the next Y-junction, take the right-hand road. About 200 yards along this road, cross the stile on the left and follow the path across a marshy meadow. Another stile leads to a grassy track, with yet another stile soon after. There is a smallholding on the right. Passing a ruined barn, go straight across the access road to the smallholding and continue, downhill, alongside a stone wall. At the point where this wall turns away to the right, cross the rocky meadow towards the forest. In the corner of this meadow there is a stile which leads into the forest. There is a short, steep descent on the other side, down rough, natural steps in the rock.

From here the path can be easily followed, running downhill, crossing a footbridge, and then going across a newly built forestry road. The path comes out on the forest lane originally met with near the start. Turn left. A short way along this lane, there is the choice of scrambling down through the trees, alongside a wooden fence, to the miner's bridge, or taking the more sedate but longer route back to the junction near Coedcynheliar Farm and turning sharp right down through the trees on the same path used on the way out. Both ways come back to the bridge and a return to the pub.

⑭ Trefriw
The Fairy Falls

Lying between the river Conwy and the eastern edge of the Snowdonia foothills, the village of Trefriw was, at one time, a vital link in the economy of this part of the Conwy valley. Small ships would come up the river as far as the village and be loaded with produce, especially timber and ore, for shipment down to Conwy and then further afield. The river was also used to ferry people wanting to take the waters at Trefriw Spa, 1 mile north, and known since Roman times for its iron-rich water. The river is now much silted up and it is hard to imagine anything larger than a motor boat making the journey today.

Trefriw today is better known for its woollen mills, producing traditional Welsh cloth, and for being a centre for visiting the lakes in the hills above, either on foot or by car.

For many years the Fairy Falls has been a centre for walkers and climbers coming to enjoy this part of Snowdonia. The Fairy Falls has the feeling of the mountains and the camaraderie that goes with them. It is a substantial and solid stone-built pub at the centre of the village, beside the rushing river Crafnant and opposite the well-known Trefriw woollen mills.

Inside, the stone fireplaces and ample-sized bars, together with posted notices of music festivals and concerts, the electronic organ and, around the side, the pool table all add up to somewhere to relax and enjoy yourself after a good day on the hills. There is a Friday night sing-along and other folk events – recently a Blue Grass festival, organised by the landlord, was held in Trefriw (although this festival is now held in Conwy).

All this requires a drink and a choice can be made between Marston's Bitter, Pedigree, Ansell's Mild, draught Guinness or Dry Blackthorn cider.

A function room downstairs caters for climbing or walking parties, or any other group, and there is motel-type accommodation for groups and visitors. Theme nights are put on every few weeks in this lively pub which is clearly part of the life of the village. Good, substantial bar meals are served from noon to 3 pm every day, with bar snacks available all day, and dinner from 6.30 pm to 9.30 pm in the evenings. These include chicken and chips in the basket, jumbo sausage and chips, beefburger and chips, toasted sandwiches, beef, ham, cheese, prawn, bacon, egg and cress sandwiches or baguettes. The Fairy Falls club sandwich is famous: ham, cheese, and egg served with Fairy Falls dressing. In the restaurant, there is a full dinner menu, which includes starters such as pâté, prawn cocktail, melon, soup or smoked mackerel. The main course has a wide range of fish and meat. Sole, steak diane, chicken Kiev and gammon are only some of the items. There is also a sweet menu which has banana boat, peach melba and choc delight, as well as ice-cream and cheese. Children are welcome and there is a small part of the bar area where families can join in.

Telephone: 01492 640250.

How to get there: Trefriw is on the B5106 Conwy to Llanrwst road, 9 miles south of Conwy and 3 miles north of Llanrwst. The Fairy Falls is in the middle of the village.

Parking: There is a large car park beside the pub and cars can be left while walkers go on their way.

Length of the walk: 4¼ miles. Map: OS Landranger 115 Caernarfon and Bangor (GR 781632).

This is an invigorating walk through Gwydyr Forest to Llyn Geirionydd and back past the old Klondike lead mine. The route follows the lie of the beautiful

61

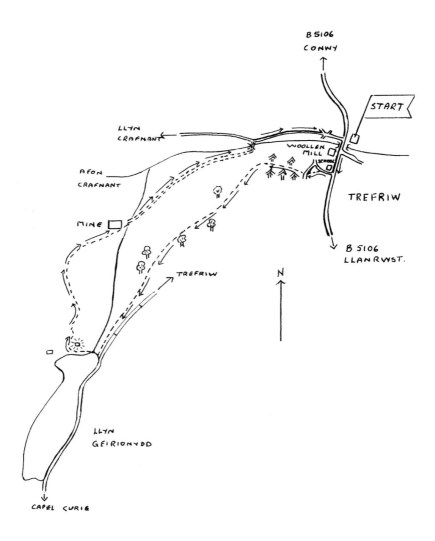

Crafnant valley, then comes to Llyn Geirionydd, a lake set amongst the hills and just one of the many to be found in Gwydyr. On the return, it is possible to see at close quarters the remnants of the Klondike lead mine – no fortunes were made here, in spite of the name!

The steepest part of the route is at the start, when leaving the village. It is suitable for all times of the year and, whilst sheep graze along most of its length, it is a good walk for dogs.

The Walk

Turn left out of the Fairy Falls, cross the bridge, and take the road on the right immediately past the school. This is the steepest part of the walk. Bearing left, carry on up the hill and opposite the church – which has a notice on the side gate saying 'Private Keep Out', turn left. At the top of this hill there is a very small wooden sign saying 'Jubilee Road', but it is very indistinct. Turn right just before this sign and go up the steep footpath which comes out on another road. Turn left here and, just past a house named Pine Mount, take the signposted path to the right. This path edges along beside a garage then enters the forest. From here, it goes more or less straight ahead through the trees and can be clearly seen. At a meeting of paths, go right, downhill, for a short distance, then take the left-hand path. At the edge of a dark, evergreen wood, cross the stile and carry on along the side of a steep hill. A metal gate is reached and, on the other side, the steady climb continues.

Two paths meet. Take the right-hand one, downhill. This comes to a wooden gate and, through it, there is a footbridge over a gulley and stream. The woods end here and the path goes past some old mining spoil. Two stiles need to be crossed before you arrive at the end of Llyn Geirionydd.

It is pleasant to walk beside the lake but the return is through the kissing-gate at this end of the lake. Walk along the stony track past the end of the lake and curve round to the left of the hillock with a stone monument on top. A grassy track leads over the brow of the hill, then goes downhill towards the valley below, tending to bear right. Crossing a wooden stile, bear right, and right again through birch and oak woods down to the old mine building.

Lead was mined in the Conwy valley for several hundred years and the last mine closed finally in the 1950s. This mine has been closed much longer. Cross the stream above the mine, then walk down beside the stream, climbing a stile and keeping to the left. The old access road to the mine drops down the valley, through the woods, meeting eventually with the lane which goes up to Llyn Crafnant. Trefriw is $\frac{1}{4}$ mile to $\frac{1}{2}$ mile further on.

To visit the Falls, turn right when you see the sign for Geirionydd. Go past the Nursery greenhouses and turn left at the telephone kiosk. Go down the hill and turn right onto a path, just after passing a house called Brookedge, go through a kissing gate and follow the path over a footbridge. This takes you down to the Falls. Follow the path through another kissing gate, turn right over a second footbridge and follow the path to where you started.

15 Roewen
The Ty Gwyn Hotel

Although the Ty Gwyn is called a hotel, it is, in fact a charming old world Welsh inn with modern amenities. Visitors and their families have the added pleasure of a river garden just across the road from the pub, beside the Afon Roe, as it comes rushing down from the hills. The Ty Gwyn is at the lower end of the attractive village, whose main street winds its way towards the hills, lined with varying styles of cottages and their gardens. It is a village much loved by artists and again of quite different character to those found in Clwyd.

This is a pub well used to welcoming walkers, as Roewen is a popular starting place for many walks. The Lees beer on offer has a distinctive flavour, quite unlike any other brew, and there are strongly held feelings about its merits amongst connoisseurs of beers, both for and against. However, whatever your reactions to it, the Ty Gwyn provides the right atmosphere for sampling a pint of 'Willie Lees' Bitter or Draught Guinness, Strongbow cider and a variety of lagers is also available. Inside, the old world bar brushes the cares of the world away and allows you to enjoy a drink and a bite to eat. Outside, on a warm and sunny day the mountain air and sound of the river flowing by make life seem idyllic.

There is a family room where children are welcome or, in fine weather, they can be safe in the river garden, but they are not allowed in the bar. Food, including hot sandwiches filled with sausage and onions or burger and onions, ham, or cheese sandwiches, fish fingers, chicken nuggets, chicken madras and vegetarian lasagne, is available. The pub is open on Monday to Wednesday from 3 pm to 11 pm and on Thursday to Sunday from 12 noon to 11 pm. Food is served every evening from 7 pm to 9 pm and lunchtime Thursday to Sunday from 12 noon to 2 pm. The cream teas are also a great draw.

Telephone: 01492 650232.

How to get there: From the B5106 Conwy to Llanrwst road take the turning signposted 'Roewen 2 miles' just by the Groes inn. The Ty Gwyn is on the right, near the lower end of the village.

Parking: There is a large car park at the rear of the pub, reached by turning right immediately beyond the pub. For those using the Ty Gwyn, the landlord is happy for walkers to leave their cars there.

Length of the walk: 4¼ miles. Map: OS Landranger 115 Caernarfon and Bangor (GR 758721).

This is an energetic walk in the Snowdonia National Park, with a variety of country and walking, from steep lanes to open hill country and pasture, with plenty of interest on the way. Some sections go through sheep country. Dry stone walls, moors, distant peaks and panoramic views of the Conwy valley add to the pleasure of walking here. There is a long, steep climb at the start which takes you up into invigorating mountain air and to a Roman road passing some notable prehistoric features.

The Walk

From the Ty Gwyn, walk up through the village. Towards the far end and past the Willow café, take the road to the right. This road starts to climb the hill almost immediately, passing a lane to the right and carrying on upwards. This is a very steep lane but, in those pauses to regain your breath, there are some fine views of the Conwy valley and the mountain of Tal-y-Fan. For a short stretch the lane levels out but do not be deceived as, shortly afterwards, it becomes even steeper than before, passing the Youth Hostel at Rhiw, a converted farmhouse. From here the far distant peaks and ranges come into view.

Beyond Rhiw, the lane becomes a cart track and then comes to a gate which opens on to the Roman road, paved but now mostly covered in grass. This road was part of the highway which led from the great Roman fort and city of Deva (Chester) to Segontium

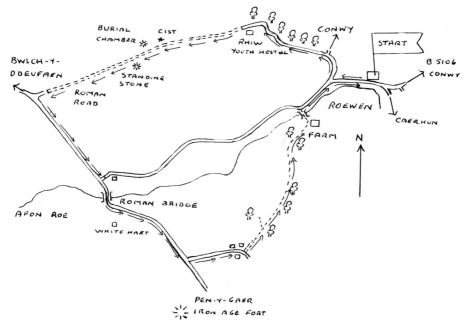

(Caernarfon). The route it took eastwards from here has been lost, especially how the road negotiated the hill just climbed, as the Romans tried to avoid steep inclines as much as possible.

As the road rises steadily, the neolithic burial chamber known as Maen-y-Bardd (Stone of the Bard) stands out prominently against the skyline to the right. This whole upland area is rich in prehistoric stone circles, burial chambers, standing stones and hill forts. Those interested in ley lines, standing stones and their significance could spend many days in this part of the country testing out their theories. About 50 yards east of Maen-y-Bardd is a stone burial cist of a later period to the cromlech. The cist was a rectangular chamber formed of rough stones and superseded the cromlech type of burial chamber. Some 200 yards beyond the burial chamber, on the left-hand side of the road and on the far side of the wall, is a large standing stone, about 7 ft high, Maen Hir (Long Stone).

The Roman road passes through another gate, then joins with a road from the left. The Roman road continues westwards from here towards Bwlch-y-Ddeufaen (Pass of the Two Stones) and crosses the hills to the coast. Do not go along the road westwards, but turn left, downhill, along the single track road. Ahead, and slightly to the right,

66

is the Iron Age hill fort of Pen-y-Gaer.

After passing a gated road on the left, an attractive little bridge over the Afon Roe is reached. Known as the Roman bridge, it is much later in origin, most probably being part of the old drovers' network of roads for herding livestock to market. Many birds may be seen here, especially in the summer, including grey wagtails, dippers and redstarts.

Over the bridge, the road rises up a short but steep hill then levels out. About ¼ mile further on from the bridge, turn left down a narrow lane. There is a small group of cottages and, just beyond the last cottage on the left, take the signposted path to the left. The old cart track leads to a gate, and, through it, the track goes downhill. Bear right where there is a fork in the path and, on reaching a gate in a wall, cross the wooden stile which is nearby. The path goes along the edge of the field, through a gap in a wall and down beside a belt of trees. A metal stile takes the path over another wall and it then continues downwards close to the fence and trees.

Climbing yet another stile, the path passes a cart track to the right and comes to a gate, which leads to an old, rough cart track going downhill through the woods. This track leads to a farm. Pass through the two gates, and then turn left, along the access road and over the river. Coming to the lane, turn right and walk back to Roewen.

16 Glanwydden
The Queen's Head

This superb pub, although not more than 2 to 3 miles from the centre of Llandudno, is in the heart of the countryside and has a top class reputation. Winner of many awards, the Queen's Head has been a finalist in the Guinness Pure Genius Pub Food competition three times, amongst other achievements. The secret of these accolades lies not only in the quality of the food provided and the bar but also in the general ambience and service which is always friendly and efficient. Great store is set by using locally grown produce whether it is Conwy salmon from the Conwy river, Conwy mussels, lamb from the farms nearby, or fruit and herbs such as fennel. The food is all the more appetising for this local enterprise, whether a bar meal or something more substantial. There is a wide-ranging menu, with some emphasis on fish, and also six vegetarian dishes to choose from.

The pub is an Ansells house and there is a good choice of beers such as Tetley, Benskins Best Bitter, Burton Ale, Thomas Greenall's Original cask-conditioned ale, Ansells Mild and Guinness. Gaymer's Olde English cider and three different lagers are also offered.

Opening times for this warm and friendly pub are 11 am to 3 pm and 6.30 pm to 11 pm every day. Children under seven are not allowed in.

Telephone: 01492 546570.

How to get there: On the A546 Colwyn Bay to Llandudno road, turn first left, at the crossroads, beyond Llandrillo Technical College. The turning for Glanwydden is about ½ mile on the left and the Queen's Head is down this road. Alternatively turn off the A470 road into Llandudno, at a roundabout, down a road marked to Penrhyn Bay. This comes to the Glanwydden turning on the right, after 2 miles.

Parking: There is a car park beside the Queen's Head but please check with the landlord about leaving the car whilst walking.

Length of the walk: 5¼ miles. Maps: OS Landranger 115 Caernarfon and Bangor, and 116 Denbigh and Colwyn Bay. The walk straddles the join of the two maps. (GR 817803).

The area covered on this all year round walk is notable for several distinctive features. Firstly, it is all within land owned by a single landowner, Mostyn Estate, and this provides a variety of land use which is 'protected'. Secondly, the route runs between two limestone ridges with a nature reserve on one and a very fine limestone heath on the other. Thirdly, the high ridges provide some excellent seascape views of Anglesey and the coast eastwards towards the Dee, as well as views of Llandudno and the Great and Little Ormes.

The Walk

The Queen's Head lies at a T-junction. On coming out of the front door, take the arm of the T diagonally opposite and walk down the road a few yards. On the left is a trackway, between some houses, which leads up to a gate. Follow the hedge on the other side, go through a kissing-gate and continue along the hedge until it takes a sharp left turn. At this point, strike out straight across the field to another kissing-gate beside a field gate. Keep beside the hedge and where a cart track bears off to the left, go right and walk along the upper edge of this field, passing a small wood, and coming to yet another kissing-gate. On the other side, follow the hedge towards a group of cottages. Two more kissing-gates and the path comes to a road by the houses at Wiga.

Turn left up the road, which soon turns into a track passing behind the houses. Ignore the yellow waymarker and turn left on the track that winds up the hill, past an old quarry. On the left is the North Wales Naturalists' Trust nature reserve. It is a reserve particularly for limestone plants

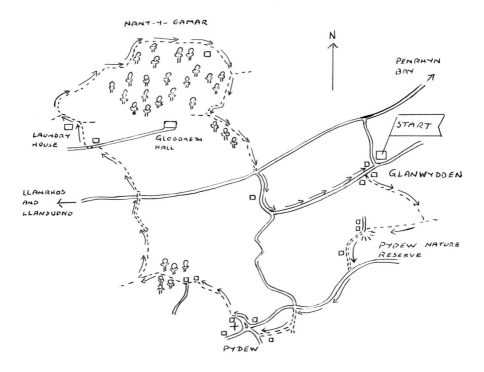

and the general habitat. Passing a cottage on the right, the track comes out on a lane. Turn right and walk ⅓ mile along this lane. Across the valley, Gloddaeth Hall can be seen. Now a boys' school – St David's College – it was for some centuries the home of the Mostyn family: a family who still own large amounts of land around Llandudno and also most of the land on which Llandudno is built.

Take the stony track on the left at the next crossroads. This passes Pydew community hall and playing field. Turn right and follow the track until it reaches a lane, turn right here and walk down to the green at Pydew. Go straight across to the chapel and walk between the chapel and the house 'Ty Capel 1929'. The path goes around behind the chapel and passes some cottages before coming to a kissing-gate. This path runs beside a wood and then drops away to the right to join a driveway. Turn left here and walk to Goedlodd Lane and the entrance to a couple of houses.

The route is straight over, down a path, past a cottage at the edge of a wood. The path goes into the wood and runs diagonally down to the far side, where there is a stile into a field. From this stile, another wooden stile will be seen half-left. Walk to this stile and then do a U-turn and walk down the hedge to the right. It may seem logical to walk straight across the field to this hedge, but the public right of way is as described, and the longer way round should be taken.

Down the hedge and through a gateway, come to a point where the hedge turns left, go straight across the field from here to a kissing-gate at the end of a hedge-lined cart track. This track meets with a road. Once a lane, road 'improvements' now allow cars to speed along it, so take care crossing. On the other side, go through the kissing-gate and walk a few yards to another kissing-gate on the left. Over the wide ditch, turn right and walk up beside the fence. Gloddaeth Hall is quite close now, and it is possible to see the older central part. At the far end of the field there is another kissing-gate and beyond the path goes diagonally up the hill directly towards the headmaster's house.

In front of the house there is a kissing-gate leading on to the driveway to Gloddaeth Hall. Turn left along the drive and in a few yards go through another kissing-gate on the right which leads into a meadow. Walk straight across the meadow to the corner of the wall which surrounds the house on the far side. Known as the laundry house, it used to be where the washing for the hall was done. Keep beside the wall up a short hill and then join a path coming through the woods. Go left to another kissing-gate and through it bear to the right around the side of the hill. Keep bearing to the right and follow a rather indistinct trackway up the side of the hill. This rises steadily towards the brow, past some gorse and thorn bushes and near the top a footpath signpost will be seen.

At the top turn right and walk over the hillside towards the wood on the top of this hill. At the boundary wall, turn left and follow it round until a house with a round tower is seen ahead. Keeping this house on the right, walk across the heath and around the grounds of the house. On the far side the land falls away towards another wood. On top of this heath there are good views of the coast both eastwards and towards Anglesey.

Walking away from the house with a tower, down the hill towards the wood, a gate will be seen in the boundary wall. Through this gate, the path drops down through the wood, turning right near the bottom and going through another gate. There is a wide view of the valley from here. At the bottom of the hill, take the path to the left which runs alongside the wall and by a row of lime trees.

Following this path across the fields and through various gates brings one to Gloddaeth Lane. Recross it and walk down the narrow lane opposite, Lon Hen Refail (Old Smithy Lane). Normally it is not very busy but it is narrow and bends, so take care. At the junction, turn left and walk the ⅓ mile back to the Queen's Head.

17 Capelulo
The Dwygyfylchi

The old coach road westwards from Conwy to Caernarfon and across the Menai Straits to Holyhead was an important link with Ireland in earlier times. It ran from Conwy's upper gate to the head of the Sychnant Pass, before dropping down steeply to the coast. At the bottom of the pass lies the little village of Capelulo, and, before the coast road was built, this small community made a living from being a staging post for travellers, coaches and other traffic going up and down the pass. Extra horses were hired out to help with the pull up the pass, and no doubt the smithy was kept busy and travellers' needs attended to. The Dwygyfylchi has continued this tradition. Capelulo is still a popular stopping off spot for travellers, and is ideally situated as a base for a variety of walks.

Two hundred years ago, part of the present pub was a smithy and part a coachhouse, and it is only comparatively recently that the pub was created. The precise English translation of the pub's name can cause some argument, even among Welsh speakers, but a definitive meaning in English of this mediaeval Welsh word is 'two circular strongholds', possibly referring to the two hillforts at the top of the pass.

Burtonwood bitter and mild are on tap, also Forshaw's, a stronger bitter than Burtonwood, and one to be specially recommended after a walk but not before! Guinness is provided, as well as several lagers, and there is the choice of Woodpecker or Blackthorn cider. In fact something to suit everyone.

A similar good choice is provided on the food side. Game pie is a well-known and popular speciality, but there is also a selection of fish dishes, vegetarian meals and omelettes, as well as pies, curries and meats. For those wanting something simpler, sandwiches, burgers and jacket potatoes with a variety of fillings can be ordered and specials are prepared every day.

Children are welcome and there is a special children's menu. Outside, a beer garden provides a sheltered and useful spot for families. Inside, old photos depict very clearly how Capelulo was many years ago before the car came.

The Dwygyfylchi is open every day from noon to 11 pm. Food is served every day from noon to 9.30 pm in the evenings.

Telephone: 01492 623395.

How to get there: Capelulo lies on the unclassified road from Conwy to Penmaenmawr. From the walled town of Conwy, take the westward road through the archway and turn sharp left immediately through the arch. At the top of the hill this road meets with the Conwy old road, turn right and after 2 miles descend the Sychnant Pass to Capelulo.

From Penmaenmawr, bear right off the main road through the town, just by the post office, and this road, after a couple of miles comes to Capelulo. The Dwygyfylchi is next to the road.

Parking: There is a large car park across the road for patrons and walkers using the pub.

Length of the walk: 5½ miles. Map: OS Landranger 115 Caernarfon and Bangor (GR 744765).

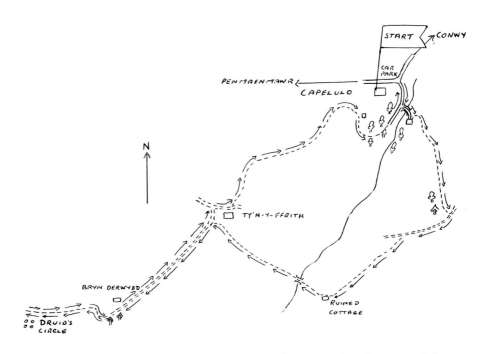

The country to the west of Capelulo lies just within the northern boundary of the Snowdonia National Park. This fine hill walk crosses exposed hill country which rises south-westwards to Tal-y-Fan and the mountains beyond, and takes in a visit to the Druid's Circle – a famous stone circle dating from around 2000 BC. After an early, steep climb the walking is good, across moorland and along grassy tracks, although it is best not to attempt this walk in poor visibility. The rare chough can sometimes be seen near the Druid's Circle and also ravens, peregrine falcons and curlews.

The Walk

Coming out from the Dwygyfylchi, turn right and then take the road to the right. Further along, cross a small bridge over a fast flowing stream and when the gateway to a large house is reached, take the path on the left which starts very close to this entrance. From here the going is uphill all the way.

The path is clearly visible and eventually rises above treetop level of the trees in the valley. A wall is reached and, at this point, go left along a grassy track, passing an old farmhouse on the right, and head for a clump of trees. The path joins a cart track coming from the left. Follow the track and a wall around to the right, until a clearly visible path breaks away from this wall and heads slightly uphill to the left.

This path initially bears left then swings to the right, crossing open moorland.

After negotiating a marshy area, bear right towards a clump of trees and a ruined homestead. Follow the boundary wall of this old homestead around to the right, and on the corner turn to the left, then, almost immediately, follow the path which strikes out across the open moor, half-right. This comes to a shallow valley, and then crosses a footbridge over a stream and a stile. On the far side, walk up the hill towards the farm in the distance.

A stile takes the path over a wall and it then goes half-left across pasture to a stony cart track. Turn left here and follow the track and directions to the Druid's Circle. An isolated house, Bryn Derwydd, in a clump of trees, is passed and shortly afterwards you turn sharp right up to a gate. On the far side, bear left. Ahead, in the distance, can be seen the long ridge of Tal-y-Fan.

By following the wall, a signpost will be reached, the left hand marked 'Public Footpath' and the right hand 'Druid's Circle'. The latter path crosses a heather and bilberry moor and shortly afterwards the stones of the circle will be seen on the skyline.

The circle is known locally as Meini Hirion (the Long Stones). It has a double ring of stones and its purpose is unknown. In 1960, excavations revealed the burnt remains of a young girl, suggesting that a sacrificial ritual had taken place.

On the return, retrace your steps, past Bryn Derwydd, to the stony track by the farm. Head down this track towards the farm, but, before reaching it, bear left along a grassy track which heads away from the farm. This track goes across the hills, eventually bearing right, downhill, and coming to a wall. Go to the left, alongside this wall, crossing a very marshy spot, and further on, by a prominent thorn tree and where the wall turns away, keep straight on. This track falls away downhill in zigzags towards the wooded valley, and then swings around to the right past some cottages. Keeping these cottages on the left, walk down the cart track through the woods and back to Capelulo.

18 Nant Peris
The Vaynol Arms

The Vaynol Arms has the distinction of being the nearest pub accessible by road to the summit of Snowdon. The Summit Hotel itself requires a train ride on the mountain railway, or the expenditure of a lot of energy to reach it. Lying at the very base of the Snowdon massif, the Vaynol Arms, very appropriately, is well connected with climbers and walkers. The pub has a new landlord and at Easter he will be taking in guests. There will be a choice of en suite rooms or a 'Bunk House' for walkers.

The pub's bars cater for three separate groups of people. The Climber's Bar, as its name implies, is the one for outdoor people. It has a tiled floor to cope with climbing and walking boots, a pool table, and is decorated with photos and pictures of famous climbs and climbing groups, as well as the equipment used. In the lounge, boots are taboo and this is a place for a more restful drink and meal. It is decorated with photos of Nant Peris showing how it was around 100 years ago. The Caban Dinorwig is a family room where children can make themselves at home. No pub in these parts would be complete without some reference to slate quarrying and in the Caban there are many items of interest connected with the quarry, all out of reach of little hands. It is a small museum in itself.

Outside, there is plenty of space to enjoy a drink or meal in the sun, surrounded by the mountains and next door to the ancient church of St Peris.

Before the vast slate quarries at Llanberis started to operate on a large scale, Nant Peris was the centre of the community in this part of the valley. Close to Dolbadarn Castle and at the bottom of the Llanberis Pass, the Vaynol Arms is a traditional Welsh inn. It is a Robinson's pub and serves Robinson's Bitter and Mild, both real ales, and also Cock Robin Bitter, draught Guinness, Hartley's XB cider and lager.

As the place is used to climbers and walkers with hearty appetites, and the landlord is also a chef, there is a good, reasonably priced menu available, ranging from soup, jacket potatoes with a variety of fillings, toasties, salads and ploughman's to full à la carte. The Kiddies Corner section provides children's favourites.

The Vaynol Arms is open all day from Easter to the end of September and in winter, seven days a week from noon to 3 pm and from 6 pm to 10.30 pm, with meals being served from noon to 2 pm and 6 pm to 9.30 pm.

Dogs will have to wait their turn outside.

Telephone: 01286 870284.

How to get there: The Vaynol Arms lies beside the A4086, Caernarfon to Capel Curig road, about 2 miles south of the terminus for the Snowdon Mountain Railway in Llanberis.

Parking: There is a large car park at the rear, which is entered around the southern side, close to the National Park building.

Length of the walk: 3 miles. Map: OS Landranger 115, Caernarfon and Bangor (GR 606584).

The walk passes through the edge of the giant Llanberis slate quarry – a way of life now gone but the area's life-blood 100 years ago, when several thousand men were employed. The extent of this labour can be appreciated on this walk. There are marvellous views of the Llanberis Pass, Llyn Padarn, Dolbadarn Castle and Snowdon itself, together with its equally impressive surrounding mountains. In the summer, a glimpse of the mountain railway can be had. On a fine day, photographers can have a field day! This walk has a long, steady uphill stretch but is quite safe and suitable for all times of the year, except in icy conditions. It is important to wear well-soled footwear, with a good tread, as slate can become slippery.

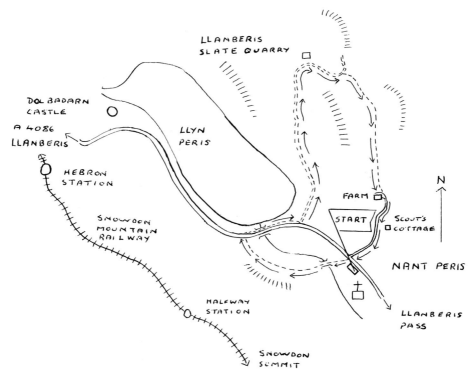

The Walk

From the Vaynol Arms, turn left down the main road for a few yards, and then left again, beside the telephone kiosk. The path runs across a meadow, through two kissing-gates to a gated, slate bridge over the fast flowing Afon Nant Peris. Walking alongside the river, the towering crags on the left are home to ravens and choughs. A dam is reached, walk around it and along the access road to the main road.

Cross the road and walk along the pavement to the right, with Llyn Peris on the left. After several hundred yards, there is a wide roadway on the left which leads steadily but quite steeply, in places, upwards. Well surfaced with slate chippings it is safe and comfortable walking, even if a little sharp for dog's pads. Take the stile to the left, and from here the track rises more steeply.

The views get better and better as you climb the side of the mountain. Below and beyond Llyn Peris Dolbadarn Castle stands out well. A ruin now, it was one of the castles of the Welsh princes in the early 13th century.

The slate from Llanberis has a fine purple tint to it and, from the higher vantage points, the great effort that went into this industry becomes quite clear. Higher still, looking across the valley to the mountains opposite, in the summer months when the train runs, the smoke from the train chuffing slowly up Snowdon can sometimes be seen. From this level, the mountain crags look even more impressive and photogenic than from down below.

The track swings around to the right and now you look directly up the Llanberis Pass, again a spectacular view. On another bend to the left, a wooden stile over a wire fence will be seen on the right. On the far side, the path is clearly visible. There is a short, flat section, then the path falls away through the slate waste. In damp weather the slate can be slippery, so take care. Slow and steady is the way to go. When the path was re-walked in the spring of 1999, it was found that part of it had crumbled away. If the path is not repaired when you visit, please proceed with caution and return the way you came if it proves to be impassable.

Eventually the path comes out on to open, grassy mountainside, with flagstones set in along its way. Bracken grows profusely here but the way should be clear to see. Cross a footbridge, go through a gate, with another footbridge beyond, over a particularly rapidly flowing little stream.

Crossing the meadow, a stile on the far side brings the path close to a farm. Walk down the gated access road, passing by a cottage, used as a Boy Scouts Association centre. At the bottom, turn right and walk back to the Vaynol Arms.

Rhydd Ddu

The Cwellyn Arms

19

The Cwellyn Arms lies at the base of Snowdon, on its western side, and has unrivalled views of the mountain. It is close to the start of one of the several routes regularly used to reach the summit, and, as might be expected, is a centre for walkers, campers and climbers, as well as tourists. Nearer to hand there are many walks in the foothills and forests and, outside, the bicycle racks for mountain bikes cater for the increasing popularity of that sport. The large forest campsite in Beddgelert Forest also swells the numbers making use of the pub, especially in the summer.

In keeping with the camping theme, there is a barbecue area at the side, used when the weather is fine. Nearby, a children's adventure playground which is open all the year round keeps the children happy. Inside, the warming fire is always a draw in this high country and provides a snug and cosy atmosphere for a drink and something to eat at all times of the year. A family room means that there is also somewhere for the children indoors. There are two en suite rooms to let as well as a two-bedroom cottage.

The Cwellyn Arms is a freehouse and open all day, all year round. The beers available change regularly but, typically, there is Worthington Best, Stones, Bass cask ale, Bateman, Beamish stout, Guinness, Dry Blackthorn and sweet Autumn Gold ciders, together with lagers. The Cwellyn Arms is just outside the Sunday 'dry area' that is still in force in parts of western Wales, so is open on a Sunday.

In the restaurant, charcoal grilled steaks, honey roast ham, garlic beef and trout are served and there is a daily 'specials' menu. Vegetarians and children are not forgotten either. Bar meals include an appetising selection of home-made soups, pies, pizzas, and salads. Food is served from 11 am to 11 pm.

Telephone: 01766 890321.

How to get there: Rhyd Ddu is on the A4085 Caernarfon to Beddgelert road and the Cwellyn Arms stands next to this road at the northern end of the village.

Parking: There is a car park immediately in front of the pub, just off the main road. Parking is fairly limited and it is advisable to check with the landlord if planning to leave the car for any length of time. Alternatively, there is a large National Park car park at the other end of the village, several minutes' walk away from the Cwellyn Arms.

Length of the walk: 5½ miles. Map: OS Landranger 115 Caernarfon and Bangor (GR 570528).

The whole area at the base of Snowdon is true hill walking country and provides a chance to stretch one's legs and fill one's lungs with fresh mountain air. This walk covers the foothills of Snowdon and also takes in part of Beddgelert Forest, which in recent years has become colonised by a variety of coniferous forest birds, such as crossbills, siskins and redpolls.

The Walk

From the Cwellyn Arms, turn left then left again up the B5418, signposted to Nantlle and Pen-y-Groes. Go along this road ¼ mile, then on a right-hand bend, go left and then through the small gate on the right, and follow the cart track running across the low-lying country around Llyn-y-Gadair. The route is marked to 'Pennant', with white arrows. Crossing a stream, the path comes to a stile. On the other side, bear left, the path rising over a low shoulder and heading in the direction of Beddgelert Forest which can be seen across the moor. The ground can be very wet and boggy over this part of the route, especially where a small stream has to be negotiated.

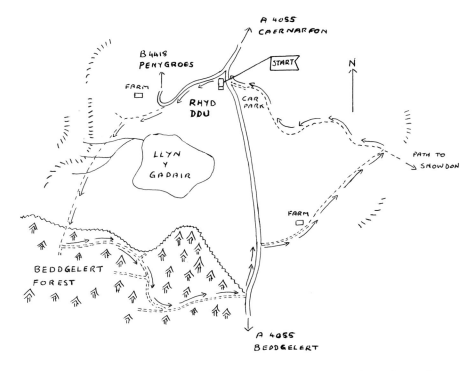

After about ¾ mile, a wooden stile is reached and from here the path goes a short distance uphill to the boundary wall of the forest. There is a gap in the wall and a clearly defined track runs downhill from here, through the recently cleared forest which will be replanted in a year or two. Just before reaching some large boulders, take the track to the left which again drops downhill, parallel to the edge of the forest. Initially downhill, it then rises up and swings to the right. At the next junction of forest roads, keep straight on, then at the following junction, turn left and walk down to the A4085.

All along this part there are good views of Snowdon and its surrounding mountains, the western side being less rugged than the three other sides. Photographers can get some good shots from this vantage point.

Coming out on the main road, turn left. This next stretch is one of the very few in this book where there is need to walk down an 'A' road. The next ¼ mile along the road does not have a pavement and care must be taken. After ¼ mile, a farm entrance, on the right, is reached. A clearly marked public footpath sign will be seen directing walkers to Snowdon. Go up the entrance road to Ffridd Uchaf Farm, bearing right past the farm buildings, then through a small metal gate, keep to the left and go uphill for about ½ mile.

The path to Snowdon will be met with coming up from the left and Rhydd Ddu. Turn left and walk back to the northern end of the National Park car park. At the other side of this car park there is a cart track which leads down between the cottages and houses towards the village. It meets with the main road and there is a short walk back to the Cwellyn Arms.

20 Beddgelert
The Tanronen Hotel

Beddgelert lies in the heart of Snowdonia and is well known not only for being a centre for touring and walking but also for the famous story of Prince Llewellyn and his faithful hound 'Gelert'. Beddgelert, in fact, means 'Grave of Gelert', but it is likely that the origin of the name is older than Prince Llewellyn and refers to the 6th century Celtic monastery which was located on the site of the present church and known in ancient records as the 'House of the Blessed Mary of Beth Kelert'.

For such a popular place it is perhaps surprising that there are no 'pubs' as such in the village although there are several hotels. The Tanronen Hotel serves, however, as the 'local' and in the bar you will hear as much Welsh spoken as English. It is the place where many of the village functions are held and the very fine glass bowl awarded to Beddgelert in 1993 for winning the village section of the 'Wales in Bloom' competition is displayed in the lounge, as well as many other prizes won by the village over the last few years, such as 'Best Kept Village' and 'Tidiest Village'. The hotel itself has been completely refurbished in the last three years.

The village itself lies at the entrance to the beautiful and much photographed and painted Aberglaslyn Pass, surrounded by mountains and at the meeting of the Glaslyn and Colwyn rivers. It is a place people visit to relax and enjoy the freedom of the hills and the pleasure of being by the white water rivers.

In the bar of the Tanronen, Robinson's Best Bitter and Mild are served, as well as Guinness and lager. Being a hotel, bed and breakfast is available and there is an attractive dining-room. Bar meals are served, both in the bar and in the 'Cricketer's Lounge'. This lounge has a large collection of cricketing memorabilia on display, as well as the village awards.

A friendly service goes with the meals, which are reasonably priced. Home-made soup, ploughman's and fisherman's lunches and sandwiches, as well as more substantial meals are on a menu to suit everyone's appetite. Children are welcome in the lounge but not in the bar. Dogs are not allowed in anywhere.

The Tanronen is open all day, every day, with flexible opening times.

Telephone: 01766 890347.

How to get there: Beddgelert lies at the junction of the A498, north of Porthmadog and the A4085, south of Caernarfon. The Tanronen is in the middle of the village, close to the bridge.

Parking: There is a car park at the rear. It is advisable to ask before leaving the car for any length of time. Otherwise, there is a large car park at the far end of the village, about three minutes walk away, for which you have to pay a fee.

Length of the walk: 4½ miles. Map: OS Landranger 115 Caernarfon and Bangor (GR 590481).

The country to the south of Snowdon is greener and 'softer' than the more barren mountains to the north. This hill walk follows the course of the old Welsh Highland railway track through the Aberglaslyn Pass, then goes up Cwm Bychan and over the top of the hills into the valley on the far side. There is plenty of good walking, and interest on the way, whether the old railway, the river, the copper mines or the views. Take a camera!

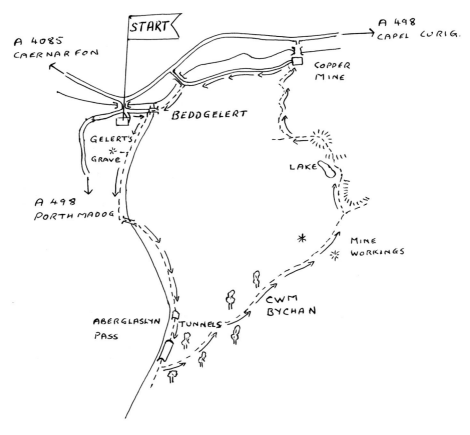

The Walk

From the Tanronen, cross the road and walk along beside the river. This access road ends at a footbridge and, just before it, there is a waymarked path to Gelert's grave. This well surfaced and well used path runs along beside the river. Do not go to the grave, unless you particularly want to make this short diversion. The route itself carries on beside the river, through a gate and across a meadow to a clump of trees. Go through another gate and head for the old railway bridge that crosses the river. This is part of the old Welsh Highland railway which in the early part of the century ran from Caernarfon to Porthmadog. There are moves to re-instate it, but, for the near future, all that remains are the trackbed, bridges, and tunnels.

Crossing the bridge, follow the trackbed to the right, alongside the

86

rushing river Glaslyn as it enters the pass of Aberglaslyn, a noted beauty spot, which Turner painted on his tour of Wales. There are two short tunnels, then a long and very dark one to walk through, with only the tiniest window of light at the far end. The ground underfoot is quite even through the tunnel and if one walks slowly and carefully there is no danger. For those who have a horror of dark places, there is a rough path around the outside of the tunnel, close to the river, which involves some scrambling and which rejoins the track at the far side of the tunnel.

Coming out into daylight again, turn left up Cwm Bychan. The clearly seen pathway rises up the cwm through some lovely woods and beside a mountain stream. Sweet chestnuts, oaks, and beech are the commonest trees here and provide wonderful colours in the autumn. Further up the cwm the path goes over a rocky outcrop and crosses a stream. The cwm narrows above here and some old trial levels of the copper mines are reached, together with the remains of a line of ropeway pylons, used to carry the ore to a collecting point below, close to the end of the tunnel. This experimental transport system was built at the beginning of the century.

From here upwards it is important to follow the directions carefully. An old turntable for the ropeway is passed. At this point, keep to the right-hand side of the cwm. Another copper working is passed, then another on the right, and about 100 yards further up the track appears to split into two. Take the left-hand fork around the base of a small hill on the right. A small lake is reached. Keeping the lake on the left, follow the path up a hill, and beyond the brow, there is a bowl in the hills.

Surrounded by mountains and cliffs, this is a very peaceful and private place, with only the ravens to disturb its silence. Take the path at the left-hand side of this bowl and follow it, past a marker post, downhill to the right. This is a rough zigzag track which needs some care in places and certainly good, ankle supporting boots. Near the bottom, take the path to the left which joins a lane heading back towards Beddgelert. At that point where the lane takes a sharp right hand turn across the river on to the main road, cross the stile and follow the path alongside the river back to the outskirts of the village. On the far side of the green, cross the footbridge and return to the Tanronen.

㉑ Maentwrog
The Grapes

The Grapes is no stranger to walkers, as, in the mid 19th century, George Borrow came here on his tour of Wales and noted in his book about his travels, *Wild Wales*, how he entered a 'magnificent parlour' and drank brandy and water. Other famous patrons have included Lloyd George and Lillie Langtry. The Grapes, a grade II listed building, with all these historical connections, has retained the best of the old and kept up to date with modern needs.

The two bars have a warm welcoming atmosphere with stripped pitch pine bars and furniture and, in the lounge bar, the walls have been stripped back to the original stonework. Polished wood bar tops and high, wooden backed chairs add to the appeal. There is also a ghost in attendance, who is reputed to play the piano in one of the upstairs rooms. Dressed in Victorian style black clothes with a white apron, she is sometimes seen downstairs but is considered to be friendly. Her appearances often coincide with alterations being carried out in the building. There does not seem to be any detailed history of her origins.

The Grapes is run firstly as a pub and restaurant but it also has well furnished letting bedrooms. The ales and food provided are well known in this part of North Wales and further afield. Worthington Best Bitter, Bass cask ale, Bass Mild and a guest beer are always available, also Guinness, Scrumpy Jack and Strongbow ciders. There are three guest beers and there is a role of honour behind the bar of those which have visited the Grapes.

The EKO restaurant has an extensive bar meals menu and they have a cellar restaurant with à la carte menus. They are renowned for selling ten different types of coffee. Opening times are from 12 noon to 2.15 pm and 6 pm to 9.30 pm Monday to Friday, and 12 noon to 5 pm and 6 pm to 9.30 pm on Saturday and Sunday. The bar is open from 11 am to 11 pm, except Sundays when times are noon to 3 pm and 7 pm to 10.30 pm.

Telephone: 01766 590208/365.

How to get there: Turn off the A487 Porthmadog to Dolgellau road at Maentwrog on to the A496 road to Harlech. The Grapes is in the village and fronts on to the road.

Parking: There is a good-sized car park at the rear. It can get busy and it is suggested that, if leaving the car for some time, the landlord is informed.

Length of the walk: 4¼ miles. Map: OS Landranger 124 Dolgellau (GR 665405).

This is a glorious walk along the river and up through the oak wood of the National Nature Reserve of Coed Maentwrog, providing a good variety of terrain to walk over. There are fine views of the Vale of Ffestiniog and of the Moelwyn range of mountains.

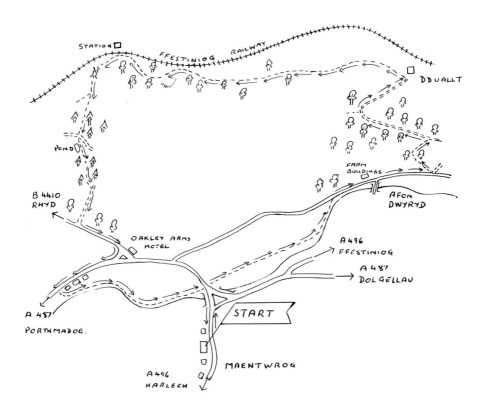

A length goes beside the narrow gauge Ffestiniog railway as it crosses the mountains. At every season of the year, this walk will provide some different pleasure and interest.

The Walk

Turn left out of the Grapes and walk down the A496 for a short distance until it joins the A487. On the far side of the bridge across the river Dwyryd, take the footpath to the right along the top of the flood embankment. This follows the course of the river and, after ½ mile, comes to a lane. Turn right and walk along the lane until some semi-derelict farm buildings are reached on the left and a metal bridge on the right. A couple of hundred yards further on, on the left, take the signposted footpath. Go through the entrance gate and then immediately start to climb the hill.

The next section is very steep and marshy, but keep going as far as a clump of trees and a water tank. Bear right here, as shown by the footpath sign on a tree trunk. A further climb is needed as far as a meadow. Keep along the right-hand side and join a surfaced trackway. Turn left and follow this trackway through the oakwoods as it rises steadily uphill. On a sharp right-hand bend, a footpath sign and stile will be seen to the left. Do not go over the stile but continue up the trackway to Plas y Dduallt.

A short way past the entrance to Plas y Dduallt, there is a large pine tree in front of the old house. Make a U-turn here, in front of the tree, and walk up to the gate on the brow of the hill. From here the path runs more or less parallel with the line of the hills, crossing open areas and then going back into the woods.

Eventually the route comes to the narrow gauge railway line. The path goes down a dip, take care here, and then rises up again to rejoin the railway line. There are fine views of the Moelwyn mountains along this stretch. A house on the other side of the line is reached, and, at this point, go downhill to a footbridge over a stream. Carry on through the woods, coming out into an open area. Two gates will be seen ahead at the edge of a conifer plantation. Take the left-hand pathway and follow the wide track through the wood, and, beyond the field gate, join with a cart track. Turn left and within a few yards take the path which goes close beside a small lake. This leads down through the woods, and over a footbridge. There is a wooden gate and then a cart track which goes down to the B4410. Turn left and walk down the verge to the Oakley Arms hotel.

Turn right down the slip road and then join the main A487 road. A couple of hundred yards further on, a group of buildings will be seen. At the far end of these buildings, there is a marked footpath to the left. This path goes over a stile and then comes on to the flood embankment of the river. Walk along the embankment to the left until the main road is reached, almost opposite the point where the walk started. Go back over the road bridge into Maentwrog and the Grapes.

22 Talsarnau
The Ship Aground

The Ship Aground is the fourth pub in this book that is reputed to be haunted. The ghost's identity as a sea captain is unusual in that, in spite of the pub's name,the Ship Aground was an old farmhouse. It does, however, look out across the estuary of the Dwyryd, and the beams in the bar are said to come from old ship's timbers, so there is a slight connection with the sea. The original slate floor in the bar and the large open fireplace are, however, reminiscent of its farmhouse origins. This is a village pub and is clearly well patronised by the locals, as well as the area's male voice choir, who have been known to give impromptu performances on occasions.

Standing on the edge of the estuary, the Ship Aground looks out solidly across the salt-marsh and river to Portmeirion, on the far bank. The famous architect Sir Clough Williams-Ellis designed the Italianate village of Portmeirion and it was, also, the setting for the classic TV series *The Prisoner* which now has a cult following. To stand by this beautiful and remote estuary it is easy to understand why Portmeirion was chosen as the location.

The Ship Aground is a freehouse, although part of the Doggett group of hotels and inns, Bass cask and Mild, and Worthington Bitter are the real ales on tap, together with a guest ale, which is changed regularly. For those who prefer something heavier, there is Guinness and, for cider drinkers, Dry Blackthorn. There is a small and congenial dining area where a very reasonably priced menu provides a good range of meals and many daily specials. Vegetarians are well looked after and also children's needs. Children are welcome in the large TV room or they can, in fine weather, play in the large garden outside.

Telephone: 01766 770387.

How to get there: Talsarnau is on the A496 coast road through Harlech. The pub is beside the main road.

Parking: There is a very spacious car park at the rear but it would be appreciated if walkers sought permission from the landlord before parking for any length of time.

Length of the walk: 4¼ miles. Map: OS Landranger 124 Dolgellau (GR 612361).

The variety of terrain that is found in North Wales is highlighted by this walk. This beautiful estuary is always a place of wide views, with the evocative smell of sea and salt-marsh, against the backdrop of the high and far-reaching mountains. The walk is quite different in character to hill walking but is no less exhilarating. Inland, the country is very little changed from earlier times – many of the ancient woods have not been cleared as they have in other more populated parts. The wooded valleys are different to those in Clwyd, deeper and with the high mountains closer, giving a more enclosed feeling.

The Walk

Starting from the Ship Aground take the road beside the pub which runs down towards the estuary. Cross over the Cambrian Coast railway line and then go through the gate on to the sea wall. There is a rickety stile, on the left, which leads on to the top of the sea wall, but this path is overgrown with thistles and nettles and it is easier to walk along the trackway at the base of the embankment, provided the tide isn't in!

After about ¾ mile the track turns inland, alongside a river flowing into the estuary – the Eisingwy. Cross the railway line again at the crossing and go straight ahead to the A496 road at the river bridge.

Directly across the main road, the B4573 runs inland, signposted 'Harlech'. After walking through the little village of Glan-y-Wern and along the B4573 for about ¼ mile, take the lane to the left. This narrow lane follows the course of a rushing stream and passes a waterfall. Continue along this lane to the left, through the village of

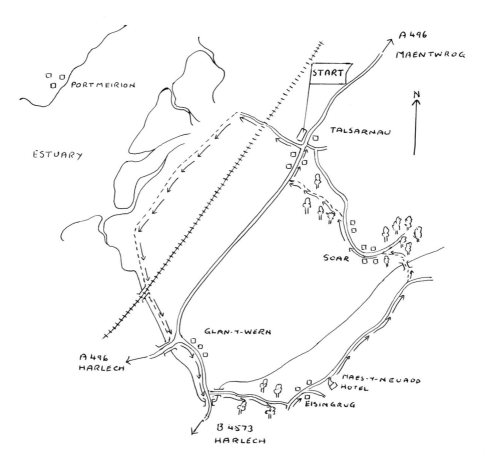

Eisingrug and past the country house hotel of Maes-y-Neuadd – the old manor house – and recently quoted by a retiring A.A. inspector of hotels as his favourite hotel amongst the hundreds if not thousands he had visited in his working life. There are marvellous views from this lane of the mountains, including Snowdon, and, also the deep wooded valleys that are a feature of the scenery in this part of Meirionnydd.

Following the lane downwards, at the bottom, take the path on the left which runs across the meadows. Stone flags are laid in places as this can be a damp spot at all times of the year and waterproof footwear will be appreciated. Across the footbridge, the path climbs up through the oakwoods, coming out at Soar, another tucked away community. The woods here at Coed Allt are under the management of the Woodland Trust as being a particularly good relic of the old sessile oakwoods which at one time covered most of North Wales.

Through Soar there is a group of houses with a playground on the right. Beyond these houses, take a signposted footpath to the left as the lane starts to descend. This path goes down through the woods and comes out on the A496 at the far end of the village from the Ship Aground. Turn right for the pub.

23 **Tremadog**
The Golden Fleece

In the early years of the 19th century William Madocks conceived the idea of reclaiming the vast estuary of the Glaslyn and turning it into farmland, by building an embankment across its mouth. This embankment now carries the A487 and the Ffestiniog railway across the river. On the reclaimed land, he laid out the town of Tremadog and, later, Porthmadog.

At that time it was hoped that the main port for Ireland would be located at Porth Dinllaen on the Lleyn peninsula, and, as the main road to the Lleyn ran alongside the Glaslyn estuary, Madocks saw the potential of creating Tremadog as the last staging post on the way to Ireland. He hoped that the town would thrive from the traffic passing through, but, in fact, Holyhead was chosen instead. This explains why Tremadog is clearly laid out as a purpose-built town in the shape of a T.

Work started in 1805 and the result can be seen today, virtually unaltered. The square had the main Irish road running along the top of the T, with hotel, inns, houses and shops all provided. The Golden

Fleece faces the spacious and attractive square, backed by the mountain.

From the outside, the Golden Fleece looks similar to the other houses in the terrace but, inside, it is especially welcoming and unusual. The bar, or 'cave' is a stone vaulted cellar type room, and the wood panelling, black beams, stone chimney breast, settles, and old glass panelled alcoves all add to a unique pub. The informal and friendly atmosphere means it is a meeting place for many people from miles around.

The snug provides another cosy and old world place to enjoy a good drink and a meal. Originally known as Auntie May's room, it was the sanctum where a previous owner entertained her favourite customers and the inn also now has three en suite rooms available, plus a self-contained flat with a separate entrance.

Tremadog being a notable centre for climbers as well as walkers, a covered courtyard at the back of the pub is the place where they can enjoy a jar and a bite to eat without having to take off their wet weather gear. Children are also welcome in the courtyard and in the games room. Across the yard is the Bistro. In the not too distant past, this part was used by Breton onion sellers to store and prepare their onion strings, before setting out around the area on their bikes to sell the onions – still a childhood memory for many. Tremadog is also the birthplace of Lawrence of Arabia.

Being a freehouse, there is a large selection of real ales including Bass cask, Theakston Best Bitter, Theakston Mild, Bass Mild, M&B Mild and Tetley and Stones Bitter. Guinness is there and a selection of lagers.

Bar meals are a treat, served from noon to 2 pm and 6.45 pm to 9 pm. There is a wide selection from simple items such as soup, pâté and French bread and ploughman's, to more substantial offerings of meat or fish dishes and vegetarian meals.

Pub opening times are from 11.30 am to 2.30 pm and 6 pm to 11 pm.

Telephone: 01766 512421.

How to get there: Tremadog lies at the junction of the A498 and A487, north of Porthmadog. The Golden Fleece faces the square in the centre of Tremadog.

Parking: There is no time limit on parking in the spacious square outside the Golden Fleece or nearby streets can be used.

Length of the walk: 3¾ miles. Map: OS Landranger 124 Dolgellau (GR 562402).

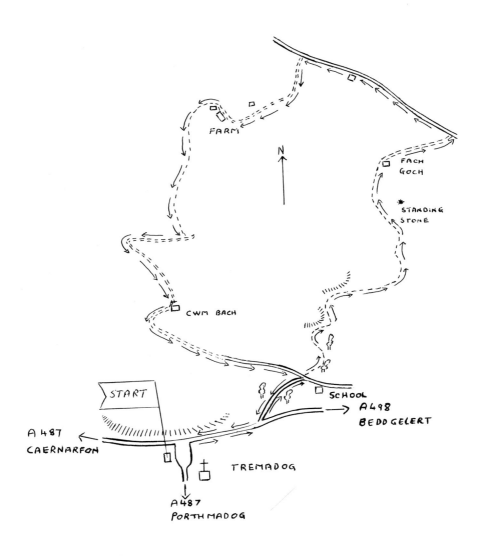

This is a hill walk across rocky and open country, covering a variety of terrain. It is fairly energetic in parts and will provide a feeling of achievement when the Golden Fleece comes into view again. There are some fine views of the estuary and the coastal region from the higher ground.

The Walk

Across the square, take the A498 road to the right. A short way along, and opposite the garage, go up the lane to the left. This passes the Ysgol Steiner Eryri school. On the bend of this lane, there is a kissing-gate and footpath sign to the right. The path beyond rises very steeply up a series of steps, beside a fence. It crosses a stile and bears left beside a stream. Crossing over the stream, a further series of rough, rock steps needs to be climbed, as the path goes through the wood. Finally a gate is reached which leads on to the mountain. Rocky crags are passed on the left, which are popular with novice climbers. The path goes around these crags to the left, beside a wall. Do not go through the opening in this wall, but keep left and at the end of this wall go right, and the path eventually comes out on to open country with panoramic views of the estuary of the Glaslyn and the conical shaped mountain of Cnicht straight ahead.

Go through a gateway, along a grassy cart track, beside a low stone wall, with a standing stone in the field to the right. The farm, Fach Goch, is reached and down the access road and through several gates, the route meets with a mountain road. Turn left and walk along it, passing a lonely cottage on the way. There are further fine views from here across wide stretches of country.

About 200 yards beyond a gate across the road, turn left through a gate at the entrance to a farm. This track leads past a farmhouse as it curls around to the right then swings left up to some old farm buildings. To the right of the buildings there is a field gate and immediately on the other side go down the cart track on the left. This track becomes grass covered as it bears to the left over the flank of a hill, and down to a gate. From here the path becomes a little indistinct, but by walking straight ahead, another cart track will be met with. This rocky track zigzags downhill, coming to a gate at Cwm Bach farm. This gate may be secured but the public right of way passes through the edge of the farm and the gate can be climbed. At the far side, walk to the right through the yard and down the farm access road until the lane by Ysgol Steiner is met with. From here, return to the Golden Fleece.

24 Criccieth
The Prince of Wales

Criccieth has the great advantage for a seaside town of being set on a south-facing hillside, so that the green and promenade catch as much of the sun as possible, as well as having a magnificent view of the far mountains across the bay. The town is dominated by the ruined castle on its castle mound. Originally built by the Welsh, it was taken over by Edward I in the late 13th century and made part of his overall strategy to conquer the Welsh. Edward also granted a charter to the town during his reign, which clearly illustrates the age of Criccieth.

Known in Criccieth as Tafarn y Maes (Inn on the Green), the Prince of Wales is at the centre of the town. The pub faces the green and, like Criccieth itself, has an old world charm about it. Inside, the dark wood, the William Morris style wallpaper, and wooden backed settles all add to the feeling that this is a pub where one can enjoy a quiet pint and an unhurried meal. The bar with its old style shelf for glasses above it, and the cast-iron fireplaces with tile surrounds provide a further link with times past, earlier this century.

This is a Whitbread pub, and there is an excellent range of real ales on offer. There are always two and generally three ales at the ready. There is, for example, the especially popular Castle Eden at 4.8%, as well as Boddingtons at 3.8%. There are also guest bitters available and Special Mild for those who are not real ale adherents. Murphy's Irish stout and Guinness provide a choice for the 'heavy' drinkers and Strongbow is there for cider lovers. Stella Artois and Heineken complete the list.

Bar meals are provided and are largely based on a daily menu. Brunch is one item that catches the eye, but there are many other offerings, such as chicken and broccoli bake, or chicken cordon bleu, as well as vegetarian dishes and children's portions. Families with young children have an area set aside from the main bars where they are welcome.

Opening times are from 11 am to 3 pm and 6 pm to 11 pm, every day.

Telephone: 01766 522556.

How to get there: Criccieth lies on the A497 Porthmadog to Pwllheli road. The Prince of Wales is on this road, facing the green.

Parking: There is parking on the roads nearby or there is a fee paying car park whose entrance is at the lower side of the green, close to the railway line.

Length of the walk: 5 miles. Map: OS Landranger 123 Lleyn Peninsula (GR 500382).

This is an easy walk with no severe uphill stretches, and it is largely on the flat all the way. It has a bit of everything, countryside, woodland, river and seashore, as well as Criccieth Castle and the historical interest of Lloyd George's former house, his boyhood home, and the museum devoted to his life and times. Throughout the whole route there is plenty of natural historical interest too, with the chance of seeing dippers and kingfishers on the river, many woodland species, and sea birds and waders on the shore.

The Walk

Starting from the green, walk along the main street in the direction of Pwllheli. A short distance out of town, a narrow lane goes off to the right, just by a lodge. Walk up this single track lane, passing, near the top, Bryn Awelon, once the home of Lloyd George but now a nursing home. Turn right at the junction and, shortly afterwards, take a pathway that goes through the small housing estate on the left. At the far end, turn right and walk to the top of the estate and through a kissing-gate to the B4411. Take care along this busy road.

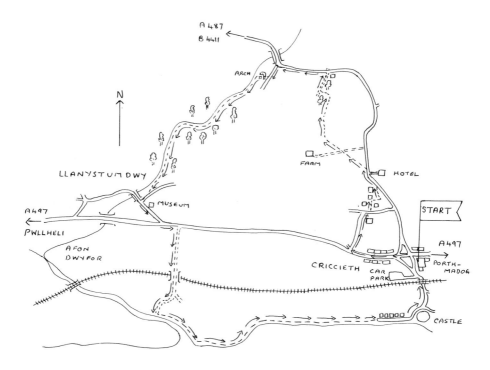

After about ¼ mile, take the path to the left through a kissing-gate and which is signposted. The route is to the right at 45° across the meadow. By walking directly in line with the end of the far ridge and where it drops down in a V, the path will be found. This very marshy area has slate slabs set in it at intervals and these will give a guide to the right direction to take.

A cart track is crossed and the path continues diagonally across the meadow to the corner of another meadow. Go through the kissing-gate, along the wall, and then through another kissing-gate. From here the path runs beside the wall and then enters a wood with an undercover of rhododendrons. Shortly afterwards a stony driveway is reached. Turn right and walk to the main road.

Turn left along the B4411 and, after about ¼ mile, turn through the farm entrance, just before the bridge over the river Dwyfor. A cattle grid is crossed and then, on the right, a path goes into the woods, through a stone arch and down to the river bank. This favourite walk of Lloyd George goes alongside the river and through the woods. The changing seasons never fail to provide a new sensation when walking down this stretch. Nearing Llanystumdwy, the path rises, passing the secluded grave of Lloyd George and the memorial to him, designed by Sir Clough Williams-Ellis, the creator of Portmeirion.

Turn right at the cottages and walk to the main road. Turn left through the village, passing the entrance to the Lloyd George museum, then his boyhood home, opposite the Feathers Inn. Carry on through the village and, about ¼ mile beyond the last houses, a cart track on the right will be seen. This track crosses the railway line and goes across low lying water meadows which are rich in flowers and birds. On sunny days in the summer, a soft and pleasant breeze blows across these meadows from the sea, adding to the pleasure of the walk. At the fork, take the right-hand way and this leads down to the estuary of the Dwyfor.

By following the clearly seen track along the shore line, a return to Criccieth can be made. Criccieth Castle will be seen ahead and there are fine views across the bay to the mountains of Snowdonia. At the end of the path beside the sea, a kissing-gate leads to the promenade. At the far end, go around the base of the castle mound, over the level crossing and to the green.

Llanbedrog
The Ship Inn

The Ship is a cheerful and outgoing place, very busy in summer and, in the winter, a haven for the locals. Good food, good beer and convivial surroundings are always a draw.

The Ship is particularly proud of its reputation in using local produce wherever possible, especially seafood, such as crab and lobster, lobstering being an important industry on the Lleyn. Another highly acclaimed offering is the 'Ship traditional steak and kidney pie', made with lean steak, fresh herbs and garlic. The wide choice on the menu is reasonably priced and everyone should be able to find something to suit their taste and appetite, including vegetarians and children. All meals are freshly cooked to order.

For liquid refreshment, Burtonwood Mild and Bitter are on tap, together with draught Guinness and a selection of three lagers – Stella Artois, Castlemaine XXXX and Skol.

With the seasonal variation in demand, the Ship expands and contracts as needed. Always in use, the bar in the older part of this 300-year-old building is what used to be called the public bar, the place for a sociable chat amongst the locals with a good drink, warm in the winter and cool in the summer. The upper lounge provides a comfortable and ideal spot for a meal and a drink from the bar. The lower lounge and the extension come into their own when things get busy.

One of the great attractions of the Ship is the mass of flowers that surround the pub in summer. It is a notable feature and a gardener is employed to ensure that there is always colour to brighten up the day, whatever the weather. The large area set aside for eating and drinking outdoors in the summer is certainly a pleasure in such surroundings.

Well-behaved dogs are allowed in the bar.

Opening times are from 11 am to 3 pm and 5.30 pm to 11 pm in the winter and from 11 am to 11 pm in the summer, every day. Meals are from noon to 2.45 pm and from 5.30 pm to 9.45 pm.

Telephone: 01758 740270.

How to get there: Llanbedrog is on the A499 Pwllheli to Abersoch road. At the crossroads in Llanbedrog, turn right on to the Aberdaron road. The Ship is at the far end of the village.

Parking: There is a large car park, whose entrance is just beyond the pub.

Length of the walk: 3½ miles. Map: OS Landranger 123 Lleyn Peninsula (GR 321318).

This is a fine and exhilarating walk around the heather and gorse covered headland at Llanbedrog, with fine views across to Abersoch and the St Tudwal's Islands. The bay is a notable sailing area. On the other side of the headland, the views southwards are, on a clear day, as far as St David's Head, in Pembroke.

The Walk

From the Ship, turn right down the village street and, at the Peniel chapel and village post office, turn right. Follow the road which then becomes a track, where it bears right, take the left-hand narrow path, which leads to a kissing-gate, downhill to the main A499 road. Cross the road and turn right. After about 200 yards along the pavement, take the path to the left. This path climbs steadily up the hill, past a cottage, and on to a lane. Turn left and continue up the lane to a junction. Take the right-hand lane which very soon becomes a cart track, leading to the headland.

Remain on this cart track, keeping to the right. It then comes out to the open part of this beautiful headland, with views of Abersoch and the St Tudwal's Islands. Passing a house, the cart track narrows to being a path which runs through the gorse and heather. Keep straight

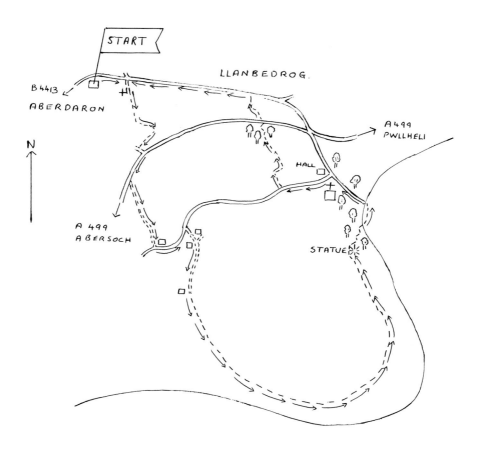

on. The clearly visible path winds around the perimeter of the headland, in parts overgrown by low gorse, so trousers are needed for everyone. Coming to the eastern side, the bracken, in summer, grows thickly, tending to obscure the path for short stretches, but the route is easy to follow, as the way ahead can always be seen.

Llanbedrog beach and Pwllheli come into view. On a rocky point, a life-size, silver-painted statue of 'Tin Man', from *The Wizard of Oz* story, looks out over the village. The statue was made from pieces of metal found on the beach. The descent from here, although a public path, is very steep. Handrails and steps are provided in places but the path has become eroded and some scrambling will be needed. It is safe, if care and some time is taken to negotiate the descent. The path eventually reaches the beach.

106

Walk around to the point where the access road meets the beach and then go up this road to St Pedrog's church hall. Turn left up Craig-y-Llan. At the top of this steep hill, take the path to the right which winds its way past some houses and then down through a wood to the main road.

Cross the road, go through a kissing-gate, passing Ffynon Trwyr Nant. At the next road, turn left and walk through the village back to the Ship.

26 Aberdaron
The Ship Hotel

Aberdaron is the most westerly village in North Wales, lying at the tip of the rocky Lleyn Peninsula. It is the place from where pilgrims set out to Bardsey Island – off the tip of the peninsula and known as the island of a thousand saints – an uncertain and difficult crossing. Sheltered from the worst of the westerly and north-westerly gales, the older part of the village is tucked away close to the south-west facing bay. It is a fine bay, with a good stretch of sand and beautiful clear water which can be quite warm as remnants of the Gulf Stream reach here. It is flanked by a rugged and spectacular coast.

The Ship, currently undergoing refurbishment, is another pub that, like so many in the remoter and more rural areas of North Wales, acts as both a hotel and a 'local'. In the bar you can find both visitors and local farmers mingling, which group is in the majority depending on the time of year. This freehouse provides very reasonably priced accommodation for those coming on holiday and also acts as a place for locals to gather, in a very relaxed and informal way. This relaxed approach is much in keeping with the character of this far-flung village and its location on the rocky Lleyn Peninsula.

The bar has a good selection of real ales, Tetley and Ansells Bitter and Mild, together with Burton in the summer, cider and three guest ales which can alter from week to week. Four different lagers are served also, and, for stout drinkers, Guinness. In the lounge bar, a comforting fire adds to the pleasure of a drink and the dining-room beyond can cope with both residents and good sized parties of people. The games area with pool table and darts adds to the easy-going atmosphere about the Ship.

In the entrance hall there is a collection of fascinating and well produced old photos of the village as it was about 70 years ago: old charabancs on an outing, boats on the beach, and the village scene with donkeys, a vital form of transport in these parts before the car made its impact. Coal was delivered from small coasters straight on to the beach and older people can remember collecting barrowloads from the beach at a price of pence for a load.

Guests need not have any doubts about the quality of the bar meals at the Ship. Bacon and eggs, omelettes, jacket potatoes, crab salads and gammon with pineapple are just a few of the dishes on offer, not forgetting the prize-winning sandwiches.

The Ship is open all day in the summer and from noon to late, according to demand, the rest of the year.

Telephone: 01758 760204.

How to get there: Aberdaron lies at the end of the B4413, which connects with the north coast road from Caernarfon and Nefyn or with the southern coast road from Pwllheli. The Ship is in the centre of the village.

Parking: Parking is limited in the village, especially in the summer, and it is best to use the private car park close to the bridge. A charge is made.

Length of the walk: 3¼ or 5 miles. Map: OS Landranger 123 Lleyn Peninsula (GR 174264).

This walk explores another aspect of the varied North Wales coastal scene, along the rugged coast of the Lleyn and with fine views of the Cambrian coast to the south. The rural nature of the area can also be clearly seen, with the characteristic small fields and low dry-stone walls, covered with vegetation. The whole area is relatively treeless due to the harsh winds that come in from the sea. The walls are a haven for many animals and birds. Keep a good eye out for slow-worms, stoats and stonechats. The shorter walk can be easily lengthened by continuing along the coastal path and taking the next footpath inland for the return to Aberdaron. There are only two steep sections, one from the beach at Aberdaron on to the cliff path, the other as part of the extended walk up the cliffs from Porth Meudwy.

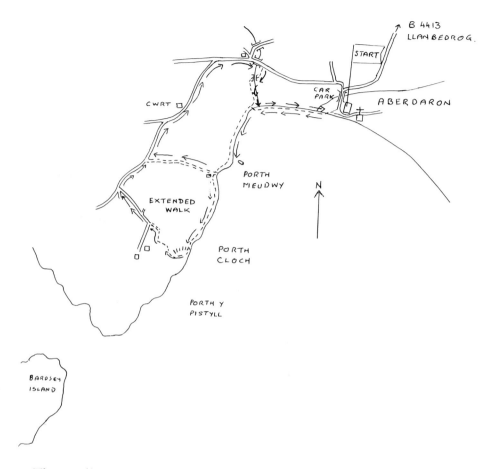

The Walk

From Aberdaron, walk along the beach to the right for ¼ mile. At the corner of the bay, where a stream flows down a small ravine, climb the steps up the cliff and then turn left along the coastal path, signposted to Porth Meudwy. There are marvellous views of the coast from here and the sea water is crystal clear as you look down on it in the calm days of summer. In the winter, the sea can be wild and spectacular as it crashes against the rocks. Lobsters are an important part of the fishing industry on this part of the coast. The whole is unspoilt and refreshing whatever the season.

After ¾ mile, the path drops down to Porth Meudwy, a small inlet with some fishing boats. Many of these inlets in the past were the main access for the distribution of goods, when the roads were poor and travel slow. Some were developed for the transportation of ore from the manganese deposits found nearby.

At this point a choice can be made, whether to take the shorter route back to Aberdaron or to add a further 1¾ miles to the walk.

For the shorter route, go inland up the access road to Porth Meudwy, which joins the narrow lane that runs back to Aberdaron. The same lane is used for the longer route on the way back.

For the longer walk, climb the steep steps on the far side of Porth Meudwy and continue along the coastal path. This section is more uneven than the earlier part and comes to Porth Cloch. A rocky area is reached, similar to a small quarry, and about 100 yards further on, with two houses in view – a red roofed bungalow and a white house – turn right, inland, and cross over a stile.

On the far side, turn right beside a fence, go through a gateway and up the left-hand side of a field around to the far corner. Go through the gateway and then through another to an old cart track which leads to a lane. Turn right, and stay on this single track lane, passing open countryside, typical of this windswept part of the peninsula. Further along this lane, the track coming up from Porth Meudwy is signposted and, from here, both routes are the same. Continue down the lane, turning right and passing the old manor house of Cwrt. Turn right and at the meeting of lanes, right again. Just on the far side of the bridge, a path to the right is signposted. This runs down the valley of the Afon Saint, and, after passing a cottage and then crossing a footbridge, the steps down to the beach are reached. Go down the steps and walk back along the beach to Aberdaron and the Ship.

Aberffraw
Y Goron

The village of Aberffraw, lying beside the mouth of the river Ffraw, is very tranquil these days, not only because the new bridge over the river takes the traffic away from its centre, but also compared with earlier times when it is thought that the village square was part of a Roman fortified enclosure, and then, after the Romans left, the seat of government for the early Welsh kings of Gwynedd. Later, Llewelyn himself, the last Welsh prince to rule over the whole of Wales, had a court here.

It is certainly hard to visualise those days when a full medieval administration was active here, with lawcourt, chancery, treasury, and royal apartments. This came to an end in 1282, the date generally accepted for Edward I's final conquest of the Welsh.

Y Goron (the Crown) is aptly named, standing as it does in the square, a memory, in name at least, of past glories at Aberffraw.

The recently built museum in the village depicts aspects of this early history of the village, and provides notes on the natural history of the area.

From Y Goron you can look out across the old bridge, the river, and over the common to the great sand dunes and the mountains of

Snowdonia beyond. It is a paradise for those who want to get away from it all or who are keen naturalists, artists, or photographers. In the cosy lounge, there is a good range of drinks on tap. Draught Guinness and Burtonwood Mild and Bitter – the latter a particularly refreshing pint after a good walk on the common and by the shore. Stella Artois and Wrexham lagers are available and for cider drinkers, Strongbow.

There is a good menu, providing a selection of sandwiches, jacket potatoes with various fillings, as well as more substantial bar meals, such as lasagne, chicken curry and fish, amongst others. On warm and sunny days, the beer garden is particularly pleasant, facing south and across to the sea, and which is currently being extended.

Dogs are not allowed in the bar but can go into the lounge, if well behaved.

Opening times are 11 am to 3.30 pm and 6 pm to 11 pm every day, meals being served from noon to 2 pm and 6 pm to 8.30 pm.

Telephone: 01407 840397.

How to get there: On Anglesey, take the A4080, off the A5. Turn down to Brynsiencyn and Newborough, just past the Marquis of Anglesey's column, and, passing Plas Newydd, carry on along the road to Brynsiencyn, Newborough, Malltraeth, and then Aberffraw. This is a journey worth taking for its own sake. Alternatively, continue along the A5, past the turning to Llangefni on the right, and take the B4422 to Aberffraw on the left.

Parking: There is parking in the village square by Y Goron or, by turning off the A4080 just before the new bridge, there is parking on the common by the old bridge. Walk across the bridge to the square.

Length of the walk: 2¾ miles. Map: OS Landranger 114 Anglesey (GR 355691).

This is an easy walk on the flat all the way and is suitable for all times of the year, but beware, as this coast receives the full force of westerly gales and there is no cover! This walk is hard to beat on a sunny day for those who are more interested in a stroll rather than a serious walk. There is so much to look at that progress can be slow. The route takes in the great dune systems that are to be found in the south-western corner of the island, both here and at Newborough. The natural historic interest is high, there being many plants unique to the sandy area, sea shells on the shore, and wildlife generally. Aberffraw is a historic village and this adds further enjoyment to the walk.

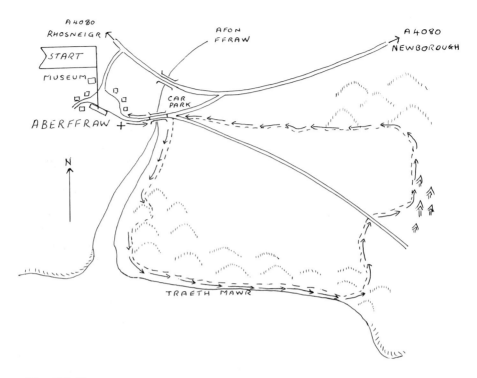

The Walk

From Y Goron, walk down to the old bridge. The river here is tidal and, at some states of the tide, sizeable fish may be seen swimming below the bridge, such as shoals of mullet in late summer. Across the bridge, follow the paths which run down beside the river towards its mouth. At low tide, the river attracts waders, such as redshanks, turnstones, lapwings and oyster catchers, as well as many gulls. Walking over the common, before reaching the dunes, the short grass, in autumn, is a mass of heart's-ease – small, wild pansies – as well as pink centaury, harebells, dove's-foot, crane's-bill, sun spurge, and fleabane amongst many other species. It will be hard to get enthusiastic botanists to finish the walk before closing time!

At the dunes, follow the pathways which run through them, keeping parallel with the river. Beyond the dunes, the beach at the mouth of the river is reached. On the far side, the low rocky coast runs northwards, but, on this southern side, the beach is backed by dunes.

Walk to the far end of the beach. There are plenty of shells here –

114

massive, old, oyster shells, mussels, razor shells, and a host of different coloured and shaped varieties. Across the water, the hills of the Lleyn Peninsula stand out – the larger ones being known as 'The Rivals'. A completely different point of interest are the planes from RAF Valley which often fly low nearby, mostly fighters of all types but larger military aircraft also use the base.

At the far end of the beach, walk up into the dunes where there is a clearly visible path. Follow the line of the wire fence, then the wall as it runs inland. At the point where the dunes end and the common starts, in later summer, the ground can be carpeted by a mass of the pink flowers of centaury. The path turns into a grassy trackway across the common, heading for the high dunes inland. Keep to the right, near the wall. The wall turns to the right and, just beyond, a single track roadway is reached. Cross straight over and bear right, towards another wall and a clump of pine trees.

Kestrels and stonechats are often to be seen here. The whole area is a mass of rabbit burrows and alive with rabbits. Take care not to step into one of the hundreds of holes and sprain an ankle! With so many rabbits, crows and ravens congregate to feed on the inevitable dead and dying. Crows are common enough everywhere but it is rare to see up to ten ravens together, as has been observed here in the summer. Large, agile fliers, they call to each other with deep croaks and barks. On this part of the common a much rarer crow may be seen. The chough has red legs and a curved, red beak and feeds on insects in the grass. Only around 900 pairs are thought to nest in the whole of the British Isles and 600 of these are in Ireland. North Wales, and Anglesey, in particular, is a stronghold of the bird on the mainland.

Walk to the base of the higher dunes, then bear left, and head back towards Aberffraw which can be seen across the common.

28 Rhoscolyn
The White Eagle

One of the great assets of the White Eagle is its position. Set on rising ground above Rhoscolyn and Cymyran Bay, it looks out southwards over the sea towards the distant mountains of Snowdonia, 20 or 30 miles away. On a clear day this is a stirring view. Full use of this asset has been made by building out the bar area, with a verandah and access to a large lawn in front of the pub. The picture windows provide a panoramic and spectacular view at all times of the year: in summer, the sparkling waters of the bay at Rhoscolyn and the misty mountains, or, in winter, the seas crashing over the rocks at the mouth of the bay, with a touch of snow on the higher mountains. This coastline is very rugged and from this point northwards the cliffs rise up to a great height.

With the strength and power of nature so close, it is comforting to come to the large and welcoming bar at the White Eagle. In keeping with its position, there is a nautical flavour to it, and particularly interesting are the accurate models of many famous sailing ships which are displayed around the bar. From the windows it is possible to see the place where the *Norman Court* – a clipper ship of similar design to the *Cutty Sark* – struck the rocks at 7.30 pm on 30th March 1883. The ship was en route from Java to Greenock with a cargo of spices, tea and oriental goods and it took rescuers almost a whole day to get to the crew and passengers so severe was the storm.

The White Eagle has a 'well ordered' feel about it as soon as one walks in, as in a well run ship. It is a freehouse and there is a good choice of beers, all being kept in excellent condition. The strongest available is Marston's Pedigree Bitter at 4.5%, Marston's Bitter and Boddingtons are at 3.8%, and also there is Marston's Iron Founders Bitter. Oyster Stout and Guinness are there for those who like their stout and, for cider drinkers, there are Symond's Scrumpy Jack and Strongbow. Carlsberg lager adds to the impressive line-up.

Away from the bar, a family room and a separate games room for pool and darts are provided. In the summer, the large lawn is very good for children.

Two separate menus are offered, a lunchtime one and another for the evening. During the day, bar meals are popular, although there is also a dining-room. The lunchtime menu has a good choice, with a notable seafood selection. Scampi, plaice, cod, tuna and pasta bake, whitebait, calamari and jugs of king prawns are some examples from the menu. There is, of course, a good range of meat and vegetarian dishes, as well as sandwiches, jacket potatoes and salads. A friendly service completes the feeling of well-being.

The White Eagle is open every day from noon to 3 pm and 6.30 pm to 10.30 pm. Dogs, if well behaved and clean are allowed to join their owners.

Telephone: 01407 860267.

How to get there: Rhoscolyn is reached by travelling along the A5 towards Holyhead. Turn left at the Valley traffic lights on to the B4545 to Four Mile Bridge. Beyond the bridge and at the brow of the hill, turn left and take the right-hand fork to Rhoscolyn. This is a narrow road and, after about 2 miles, with a church to be seen on the hill ahead, turn left down the very narrow lane to the car park of the White Eagle.

Parking: There is a large car park beside the pub.

Length of the walk: 3¼ miles. Map: OS Landranger 114 Anglesey (GR 270756).

No series of walks on Anglesey would be complete without a visit to the high cliffs on the north-west of the island. On the walk you can appreciate the grandeur of this rugged coastline and enjoy the beautiful clifftop heathland which, in summer, is full of grassland flowers and butterflies. Choughs are frequent here on the grassland and around the cliffs, as are many seabirds, ravens, and peregrine falcons.

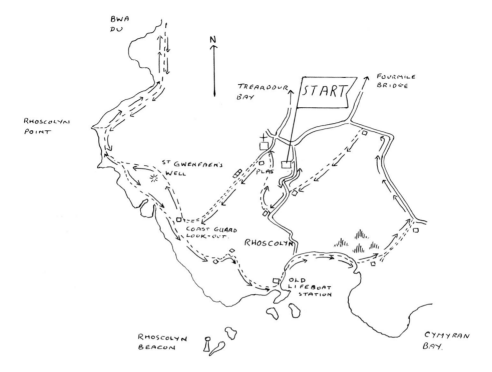

The Walk

From the White Eagle car park, turn right down the lane and follow it around several bends. On a sharp left-hand bend, next to the entrance to Ty Weryl, take the footpath signposted to the right. This means passing through the gateway to Ty Weryl and then immediately going along the footpath beside the garden.

This leads to a wooden gate and the path then continues across a meadow and over a farm access road. Passing through a kissing-gate, cross another meadow to a stone built kissing-gate. On the far side, walk towards the church on the hill. Climb the wooden stile and go down the access road to the left, passing the large house, 'Plas', and the old barns, dated 1771. This well-surfaced track goes by some houses and, shortly after, there is a kissing-gate. From here the track runs up to the coastguard look-out station which is on a rocky knoll. At the base of this knoll, on the inland side, a grassy track goes to the right parallel with the coast. Holyhead mountain can be seen straight ahead in the distance.

Keep alongside an old field wall, now covered in gorse and grass, passing across some marshy ground where there are stepping stones set in the bog. In the right season, this area is ablaze with wild flowers of many different species. Further on is St Gwenfaen's Well, surrounded by a stone parapet. This holy well is named after the nun who founded the village church at Rhoscolyn.

From the well, walk down towards the coast and Rhoscolyn Head. This a good spot to get an excellent view of the high cliffs and the coastline, with its very ancient folded rocks, and it is often possible to watch divers and lobster fishermen and climbers attempting to scale the cliffs. An extra ¼ mile along the coastal path will bring you to an archway in the rocks, and nearby there is a stone engraved 'Tyger, September 17, 1819'. This commemorates the bravery of a dog named Tyger who saved the crew of a ketch which had sunk ¾ mile offshore in a fog. The dog guided the men ashore by barking as he swam. He then dragged the ship's boy ashore, before going out to help the captain, his master. The effort was too great and Tyger fell dead as he reached the shore a second time. The grateful survivors erected the memorial in memory of Tyger's courage and loyalty.

From this point, return to Rhoscolyn Head and walk back towards Rhoscolyn along the edge of the cliffs, avoiding the deep chasms which run inland! Shags nest on the sheer sides of these inlets. The coastguard station is easily seen on its knoll. Walk up to it, and, this time, pass by its base on the seaward side, going down the hill towards Rhoscolyn.

There is a kissing-gate in the wall and, beyond, cross the meadow towards a group of houses. Climb the stone stile and walk along a walled path behind a barnlike building. The path emerges on to the lawn of a private house. The public right of way is along the hedge and then right, and not down the driveway to the house. Follow the road down past the old lifeboat station (1886) and cross the top of the beach to the new sea defence wall. Walk along the wall as far as the beach car park and then carry on around the beach to the far side of the bay.

Just before a small, rocky, headland, take the path which runs inland. This path crosses three stiles and then comes out on a roughly surfaced lane. Turn left along this lane which meets a metalled, and narrow lane. Walk down this lane to the left for about ⅓ mile and then, beside a house called 'Coedon', take the path signposted over the stile to the left. This crosses the fields and comes out on another narrow lane close to a house. Turn right and walk back along the lane to the White Eagle.

Brynrefail
29
The Pilot Boat

Just outside Brynrefail (Smithy Hill), the Pilot Boat nestles comfortably in the lee of the hill, overlooking the inlet of Traeth Dulas. The view is a typical scene for this part of Anglesey, with undisturbed fields and woods running down to the edge of quiet inlets and sandy coves.

The Pilot Boat, in fact, used to be a smithy, although the history of the pub is not well known. Certainly, now that the main road no longer runs right outside the front door and the pub is bypassed, life is a lot more peaceful and it is an excellent meeting place for walkers who are planning to walk the Anglesey coastal path. Parties from all over the country enjoy a pie and a pint here before setting out, or on their return, or it may be the local coastguards, in for a quick glass, who are at the bar.

Away from the rush of traffic and yet close enough to be clearly seen from the road, it is a good place for a quiet drink and a meal. It has recently been completely refurbished.

There are pictures of the Moelfre lifeboat and its crew. The famous lifeboat station has figured in many rescues of national interest, as the coast nearby is very treacherous. The most famous wreck, however, was long before the present lifeboat. In October 1859, the iron hulled, fully rigged sailing ship, *Royal Charter*, on passage from Australia to Liverpool, was driven on to the rocks, less than 2 miles from the pub.

Apart from being fully rigged, she also had an early type of steam engine installed, which broke down in the hurricane force winds and 452 people were lost, even though the ship was on the rocks only 25 yards off the beach, with help at hand. Divers still search for the gold that was reputed to have been on board and never recovered. Charles Dickens tells the story in his book, *The Uncommercial Traveller*. Paintings in the pub show the *Royal Charter* and its wreck.

Amongst all these nautical memories, Robinson's Best Bitter and Mild are served, also Guinness and Strongbow cider.

The newly opened dining-room is attractively set out and is available for groups and families. Children are allowed in the main bar, in the dining-room or in the lounge, where there is a pool table and comfortable seating around the walls. Dogs are not allowed. There is an extensive menu, especially for those with a hearty appetite from walking. Ploughman's, sandwiches of all sorts, and jacket potatoes are all very reasonably priced, as are the 'main' course items. Outside there is the chance to enjoy the fine weather with a drink. Certainly the views from the Pilot Boat are idyllic.

Opening times are from 11 am to 11 pm, seven days a week from March to October. November to February from 11 am to 3 pm and 6 pm to 11 pm, Monday to Friday and all day on Saturday and Sunday. Meals are served all the time the pub is open.

Telephone: 01248 410205.

How to get there: The Pilot Boat is ½ mile north of Brynrefail on the A5025 Menai Bridge to Amlwch road.

Parking: There is space to park on the old road or in the large park at the side of the pub.

Length of the walk: 3½ miles. Map: OS Landranger 114 Anglesey (GR 476873).

This is an easy walk suitable for the drier times of the year. It is quite different to the other Anglesey walks described. The farmland reaches to the low, rocky cliffs and sandy bays. Country paths suddenly open up on vistas of the sea between the trees

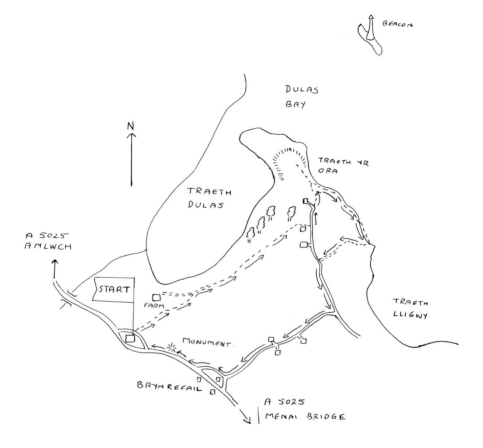

and each season of the year provides new aspects of this secluded and unspoilt place. Initially through farmland, then along the coast, the walk returns along country lanes.

The Walk

Immediately opposite the Pilot Boat, take the waymarked path. This runs along the hedge and then over a stile on the right, continuing along the hedge on the other side. There are views of Traeth Dulas from here. Cross over the concrete stile onto a cart track which leads straight on up the hill. On reaching another stile, cross the meadow, bearing left towards a shrub covered knoll. Keep along the base of this knoll and go down a short incline. The path can be clearly seen running straight ahead parallel with Traeth Dulas. Cross another meadow to its left-hand side at the far end and go down a gap in the hedge. Follow this hedge to the right and go through a kissing-gate, close to a small cottage. The path leads to a lane. Turn left and, at the next house, take the cart track to the right, then the path to the left which is at the end of this track. The path divides, the left-hand fork going to the headland at the mouth of Traeth Dulas. A diversion can be made but there is need to come back to this point to continue the walk.

Nearby are some stone steps to the beach, but the route itself carries along the top of the low cliff which in the summer may be thick with bracken. To follow the path, head towards a clump of trees. It is uneven here so take care. Climb some stone steps into a small meadow and carry along the cliff edge. The rocky coast far ahead is near the point where the *Royal Charter* struck on the night of October 25th. Climb the stile and follow the path to where it drops down to the beach of Traeth Lligwy. Walk along the beach towards the marker post at the far end. Steps lead up to this post, but do not go up them, instead, at their base, take the wooden stile which faces inland. On the other side, head inland along a hedge and around the side of a field until an old grassy cart track is found, bearing off to the left. By going along this track a kissing-gate is eventually reached which leads to a lane.

Turn left, then right at the next junction, walking back to Brynrefail. At the entrance to the village, take the old road to the right which joins up with the new road a short distance on. Walk along the pavement for ¼ mile back to the Pilot Boat, passing on the way the monument to the Morris brothers, who were born nearby in the early 18th century and who became famous in Wales and London for their own writings and the help given to other Welsh authors at that time.

Red Wharf Bay
The Ship

The Ship Inn looks out across ten square miles of sand at low tide and what must be one of the finest beach scenes in the whole country. Facing south-east, the broad sweep of the bay, from Llanddona on the far side around to Red Wharf, backed by wooded hills, lies directly in front of the pub. This is a part of Anglesey that provides great scope for walkers, for those who delight in beachcombing, for birdwatchers, or those who prefer to come and enjoy the views and sea air.

The Ship is very much in keeping with these surroundings. Long ago, the 400 year old buildings were warehouses, perhaps connected with the time when Red Wharf was a small port and boat-building centre. Later, as trade declined, the Ship was set up as a pub and is now known for many miles around, for the quality of its beers and food and for the pleasant surroundings in which to enjoy them.

The Ship is a freehouse and offers a good selection of cask conditioned beers, no keg beer being sold. The list is changed regularly but a typical selection might be Tetley Bitter, Tetley Mild,

Friary Meux Bitter, Marston's Pedigree, Draught Burton Ale, Benskin's and Dry Whitethorn cider, Guinness, and a couple of lagers, such as Wrexham and Carlsberg Export, are also available.

Even without the blazing fires in winter, the inside of the pub always has a 'warm' feel to it. On sunny days in summer, there is the chance to sit out on the green and enjoy the panorama of Red Wharf Bay. For children this is ideal and there is also a family room indoors which is popular in summertime. Instead of one-arm bandits and juke boxes there are more substantial pub activities such as darts, and this helps to make the Ship the place it is.

The food at the Ship is also of a high standard. Bar meals are available every day from noon to 2.15 pm and 6 pm to 9.15 pm, although the Ship is open every day from 12 noon to 2.30 pm and 6 pm to 9.30 pm. Each day the bar meals available are posted on a blackboard and can include, as well as sandwiches, salads and pâté on toast, such items as cottage pie, pepperpot beef with ginger, Stroganov and chestnuts, grilled gammon and pineapple, mussels in garlic topped with cheese, lasagne, and salmon and broccoli Mornay. Children, likewise, have a good choice.

Looking out across the bay to Llanddona, the modern TV mast can be seen on the hill, but in the Dark Ages, Llanddona and Red Wharf were the reputed haunt of some Irish witches. They had been set to sea from Ireland by those tired of being troubled by them and eventually were cast up at Llanddona. They frightened away the locals and settled there, making sorties across the bay on their broomsticks to further scare the locals. (Where did the widely held belief about witches and broomsticks originate?) They were finally evicted, but the witches of Llanddona are still remembered.

In more recent times and well documented, Red Wharf Bay was where the submarine *Thetis* was beached after the tragic accident in 1939 when she went down in quite shallow water off the Great Orme at Llandudno. Most of the crew were lost in spite of great efforts to save them and it was one of those tragedies which caught the attention of the whole country.

Telephone: 01248 852568.

How to get there: Take the A5025 Menai Bridge to Amlwch road. About 2 miles beyond Pentraeth, take the signposted lane to the right to Traeth Coch/Red Wharf Bay. Follow the signs down to the shore and the Ship is on the right.

Parking: At the shore there is a large public car park and, beyond, a private car park for the Ship.

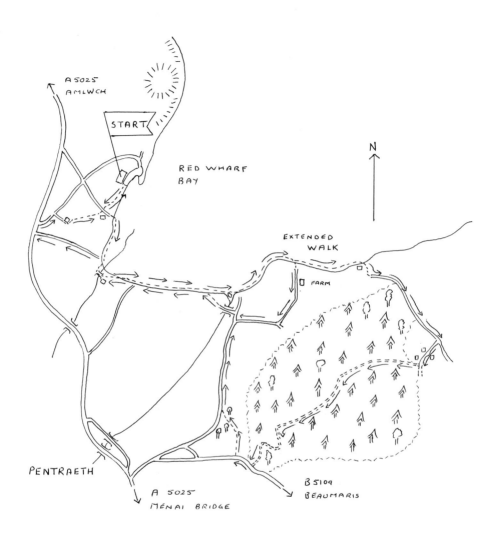

Length of the walk: Depending on one's mood there are the alternatives of either an easy stroll of about 3 miles which can be lengthened as far as you like along the beach, although the return will have to be back along the same way, or the walk can be a circular 8 miles along the beach and back through the wooded hills behind. Map: OS Landranger 114 Anglesey (GR 529811).

On the shorter walk the going is easy all the way. The longer walk has one moderate uphill stretch but otherwise the going is also easy. Care should be taken if wandering out over the beach at low tide to ensure that the tide is not flooding in around behind as it comes in fast and fills deep gullies quickly. Whether walking the shorter route, or the longer, the country and shore are particularly impressive. The walking is good underfoot and there is much of interest on the way, whether sea shells, birds, or the ancient unimproved meadows that border the vast expanse of the bay and still contain the prolific plant life that thrived in these meadows before the advent of artificial fertilisers and weedkillers.

The Walk

From the Ship take the path to the right, past a small toilet block. This leads up through the woods and through three kissing-gates to a lane. Go left on to the beach and follow the very muddy and boggy track to the right which runs around the edge of the bay. It was near here that the building of small coastal sailing ships took place.

A stone footbridge crosses a stream which runs into the bay. From here walk along the edge of the beach until once away from the muddier parts, there is scope to wander at will across the sands. The route for the two alternatives continues along the edge of the tideline, crossing another stream at low tide or, if the tide is in, making use of the old bridge, returning to the shore on the far side.

Carry along the shore, until level with a farmhouse several hundred yards inland.

For the shorter route, turn up the sandy path that leads directly past the farmhouse to an access lane. Further along, turn right down the road. At the telephone box, turn right, then left, over the old bridge and walk back to the footbridge previously used. From here, take the lane to the left and walk up to the main road. Two hundred yards to the right there is a lane on the right and a further 200 yards down this lane there is a driveway that is waymarked. At the entrance to a house, take the path to the right which hugs the perimeter of the garden. This path then leads down to the lane used earlier and, uphill from here, is the point where the path from the Ship met with the lane. Return along the same route.

For the longer walk, at that point where a turn inland was made, continue along the beach, past several entrances to properties. A small, wooden chalet is reached and, just beyond, a sandy track goes inland, meeting with a metalled lane beside a wood. This lane climbs up the hill for ½ mile, then meets with Forest Lane on the right. There are some large houses built along Forest Lane but, beyond the last one, the lane turns into a cart track. A fork is reached, go straight ahead into the wood, through the gateway.

Follow the forestry road through the wood, bearing left at the next junction which is on a left-hand bend. At the next junction, go right. The road descends the hill in a series of long curves and eventually comes to the B5109 Pentraeth to Beaumaris road. Turn right along this road, passing the end of the wood, and taking care along this winding and quite busy road.

A short distance beyond the end of the wood, there is a stone stile on the right which is signposted. The path goes along beside a hedge, then switches to the other side of the hedge through a wrought iron gate. Keeping along the upper side of this hedge, and a short distance further on, a marker post will be seen in the field, and another small post in the same field on the left shows the way down towards a wood. A simple wooden stile takes the path into the wood, bearing half right. At the far side and down a bank another simple stile will be found. Diagonally to the right, across the meadow, there is a cast iron gate in the hedge. Coming out to the lane, turn right and walk down to the telephone box. Walk back to the Ship by taking the road over the old bridge on the left and keeping to the edge of the bay as on the way out.